To my <

CARAVAN OF LIFE

John Moseley

Merry Christmas 2020
Lots of love from
Irene
X

ISBN-9798667887997

Cover design by: Phillipa Phillips
Library of Congress Control Number: 2018675309
Printed in the United States of America

As always for Gilly

CONTENTS

ACKNOWLEDGEMENTS

First and foremost my great friend Paul Duffin for as so often in my life making me believe I could do this in the first place. Having done so he then agreed to be my editor. Most of what follows would be virtually unreadable without his input and encouragement. Any remaining errors I take the full credit for myself.

Secondly, my wife Gill for supplying ideas memories and putting up with me spending hours in front of a computer screen.

Thirdly to Russell Dodd and Mark Slater for their suggestions to improve the finished article.

Finally to my very talented daughter Phillipa for designing the cover.

FOREWORD

I intended to write a book about caravanning, I honestly did. I thought that something describing the adventures and mis-adventures of self-catering holidays on a shoestring might be entertaining. however my lifelong talent for going off at a tangent dictated that I ended up writing a book about, well, I suppose me really. Even I realised that this subject matter would be of limited appeal, so I do introduce you to lots of other people along the way. I hope to entertain you and even to make you laugh sometimes, after all I have asked you to part with a not inconsiderable sum of money.

I have always considered myself fortunate to have enjoyed good health. I feel particularly privileged that, other than the odd little scare at the start of life, my children and grandchildren have been similarly blessed. I cannot begin to imagine how I would cope with the loss of a child or grandchild before I depart this mortal coil myself. I fervently hope and pray that I will never have to, for I doubt I would find the reserves of guts and courage it must take just to carry on. I can only admire the few people I have known who have faced such a traumatic event. Even so they have been changed by it forever and for this reason the royalties, if any, from my efforts will be donated to Claire House Children's Hospice on the Wirral. They help seriously and terminally ill children live life to the full by creating wonderful experiences and bringing back a sense of normality to family life. By providing specialist nursing care and emotional support they help families to smile again when life couldn't get any tougher.

A final word of warning. I have been told that some people may be offended by some of my attempts at humour. If you are one of them please believe it was not my intention to upset you in anyway. The events I outline all actually happened and the Dutch language is what it is. I could not have told this story any other way.

...AND SO IT BEGINS

Apart from a few half-remembered trips to seaside boarding houses, when I was very young, I have spent, with only a few exceptions, every holiday in a caravan. It is possible you are thinking that I have somehow been deprived. However, I'm not looking for sympathy here. I have loved it all. Friends and relatives think I must be mad, which I find slightly galling, so I do feel the need to try and explain myself. What follows is a sort of explanation. Not all of it is about caravanning but it may explain the slight madness.

I was around ten years old when we acquired our first caravan in 1969. My dad liked a bargain and on this occasion at least I think he managed to get one. Somehow he persuaded a hapless caravan dealer in Chesterfield to part with a nearly new caravan in exchange for a rather old car with some ninety thousand miles on the clock. Anyway we became the owners of a nearly new Lynton Scamp touring van.

In the mid-sixties all caravans were basic and this one was especially so. I think the internal length of a Lynton Scamp was around three metres or about ten feet in those days. Amazingly into a space which would be approximately the size of four telephone boxes they somehow created three bench seats, which converted to sleeping accommodation for four people, a dining area, a wardrobe, cooking facilities and even the kitchen sink. There were no toilet facilities.

All cooking had to be done on a two ring gas burner and light was supplied by a gas lamp over the front table, which as the van was so small also served as a heater. Water was supplied by a foot operated pump and came in two temperatures, cold or icy, depending on the time of year. You had to do an awful lot of pumping to get a very small quantity of water and the whole caravan floor bounced alarmingly whenever anyone oper-ated the foot pump. Every drop of water used had to be lugged from a standpipe by means of a plastic five-gallon plastic water carrier. Every drop of waste water was collected in a bucket under the van and carried back to a drain. Gas came from two small metal canisters carried on the front end of the caravan, the so called hitch.

My mum and dad my younger sister Jan and I from this moment on spent our holidays in this space. It is a testament to, - well all of us really, that we never had any serious fallings out. We didn't even have an awning or separate tent to create more space. At the time of writing I am sat at home in the Coronavirus lockdown. One of the reasons I think I am coping happily is that my childhood holidays have prepared me perfectly for this moment. In 1969 my mum would have been around thirty-four, my father thirty-eight and my sister seven, so we are talking about a standard family of four and of course the two younger members were getting bigger all the time.

My dad was a branch manager for the TSB the first time around. In those days TSB wasn't really a bank in the full sense of the word. It was a deposit taker but unlike a Building Society it's depositors did not own any part of it. The deposits it took were used to purchase government debt.

It didn't do any other lending and for this reason tended to be looked down on a bit by the commercial banks, which my dad understandably resented. Much later when I worked for a building society I understood how he felt. However, the mutual building societies and the savings bank movement were less hard-nosed than the clearing banks. They were undoubtedly a force for good in democratising property ownership and creating wealth for the common man. I lament their passing and am proud to say I worked there. I hope my dad eventually felt the same.

My mum like most mums in those days, didn't have a full time job, she did however work as a school meals supervisor for an hour a day. My sister and I get on very well indeed, in some ways she is also my best friend, but back then when I was ten and she was seven, boy could she be irritating!

Now, as I mentioned the car had been exchanged for the caravan, so the first priority was to get a new car to pull it with. Preferably something bigger than the diminutive Austin A40 it had replaced. When I say new car, what I mean of course is, new to us, which means an old car. Back then not many cars, with the exception of a Land Rover were designed for towing, so apart from having a tow-bar fitted you also had to make some additions to the rear suspension to prevent it from bottoming out, as they would say in a Carry On film. There were several weird and wonderful options and most of them looked like they would be more at home in a masochist's bedroom. One consisted of two hard rubber balls that were fitted inside the existing coil springs. Another was simply a set of metal leaf springs tied together, which looked like a restraining device but was in fact meant to add extra support to existing leaf springs.

First up was an absolutely knackered Ford Cortina. It had been a friend of the family's car. Unfortunately, the said friend was a sales representative of some description and it had been thrashed to within an inch of its life up and down the country for some five years before we got it. I don't think we ever went anywhere without it breaking down at some point along the route. We just knew it was going to happen. We even prepared for it by taking extra sandwiches and games to play. I lost count of the hours and half days we spent stuck at the side of the road or in motorway service areas waiting for the AA to turn up. It must have been the worst bit of business the Automobile Association ever did. I'm surprised they carried on offering us cover. The car lasted about a year, after which even my dad couldn't stand it any longer and we traded it in for a slightly newer Austin Cambridge. I believe the friend of the family, who sold us the original car, ceased to qualify for this status.

If you are ever offered a 1964 Ford Cortina DWE679B (Why is it, you always remember these things?) run a mile. Mind you, if it is still around it will be worth a fortune. It left me with an entirely unreasonable hatred of Fords which I didn't get over until my mid-twenties, when I got my own very reliable Ford Sierra.

Our first ever holiday was to Stony Stratford in Buckinghamshire. This would be around Easter-time. Nowadays, Stony is part of Milton Keynes, but in 1969 spades were only just being put in the ground and so it was just a rural market town. I've spent a lot of time in and around Milton Keynes since then and Stony Stratford is still a very pleasing place to visit. It is an attractive town, on the banks of the River Great Ouse, pretty much half-way between London and Birmingham on the old roman road Watling Street. Nowadays it is more often, if less romantically called the A5.

In the days when this journey could not be completed in a single day, the horse drawn coaches would stop overnight at Stony to rest both horses and passengers. Thus those heading up from London and down from Birmingham would meet at the coaching inns. These were the Old Cock Inn and the Bull Inn which stand opposite each other on the high street. They would of course exchange news and tales from each of England's two main cities. As the evening wore on the tales would get taller and taller as travellers got drunker and drunker. It is from this dubious method of passing on the news that we get the expression, "A cock and bull story." This is an example of the sort of thing you find out when you tour the country in a caravan

It is truly astonishing the odd things you learn, particularly if you stay on smaller sites on farms. Why is so much maize grown for example? The answer farmers prefer to give is that it is for animal feed, especially dairy cows. If you push them they will admit that quite a lot of it ends up in anaerobic digesters. What is an anaerobic digester? It is a machine that converts the said maize into bio-fuel.

Farm tractors on large arable farms are self-steering, they make maps of the fields they work in and so require little human intervention to plough a field. Combine harvesters are also self-steering and can work out which areas of fields have lower yields. This information is then used by seed drillers and fertilizer units to either add extra fertilizer, or avoid seeding these areas. I would know none of this without having spent so much time on farm caravan sites.

Caravan sites, even quite large ones, were in those early days nearly as basic as the caravans. They would have a toilet block which also housed the showers and rows of pedestal basins. Some would have pot washing areas but that was usually your lot. There were never enough wash basins or showers to cope with demand in the morning, so a queue would form which snaked round the block. There were not enough toilets either so there was a separate queue, consisting of people in various stages of desperation, hopping from foot to foot, waiting for a WC to become free.

One site we stayed on had the toilet rolls hung

on the outside of the toilet doors. I am sure this contributed to the economy of running the site, but if in your state of urgency, you forgot to collect paper on your way in then boy were you in trouble. It was not uncommon to hear stressed and dismembered voices from cubicles pleading for more paper to be passed under the door. It was also not uncommon to see people in the queue carrying their morning newspaper. This was a disheartening sight as it clearly meant that whichever cubicle they eventually went into would be out of service for some considerable time. A number of these early caravan sites had been converted from old army barracks left over after the war. They were not designed for luxury. Often the toilet block buildings did not have roofs so if it happened to be raining, you just got rained on as you reigned on the throne.

Caravan sites were places however where you always met lots of other children so there were always games of something going on. Football, or cricket or rounders' you name it. There seemed to be an unwritten rule that fathers would take turns to organise and supervise the game to ensure fair play. Teams were not necessarily restricted to eleven players each, it just depended on how many people turned up. The winner of a game of badminton was not determined by points scored but by how long two players could keep a shuttle-cock in the air for. The loser was the one who let it fall to the ground no matter how impossible the return shot might have been. I was good at this, very good, but it totally ruined my game of competitive badminton, since I could never break the habit of returning every shot, even those that would have self-evidently been out.

Organising children's games was always a dads' responsibility I suppose it gave the mums a rest for whom caravaning always was less of a holiday. In an age where women still did most of the domestic tasks, the only real advantage, from their point of view, was that they had less space to clean. Today whilst you still do see families caravanning, it seems that there are now a greater preponderance of older empty nesters than I remember back then. Modern women who are more likely to be holding down a full time job have probably quite rightly demanded a proper holiday.

A caravan holiday did however mean that you spent quality time together. You had no choice, there was no television, so evenings were spent playing cards or board games together. To seat four people at a caravan dining table you have to clamber in one by one and once you are in there, then there you must stay for the duration. The last person to sit down has to be the first person to get up, so this most accessible seat is always reserved for the cook at mealtimes. Having four people in a small caravan always reminds me of one of those puzzles I had as a child, where you could make a picture or words from tiles that you slid around a frame but you could only move one tile at a time. If you aspired to solitude this was not the place to be.

There are only three specific things I can remember from that first holiday and none of them are very pleasant. Firstly, and inevitably, we broke down, spending a few very unhappy hours at the Watford Gap service area on the way down. We had not yet learned to pack additional supplies or entertainments and there are only so many things you can I-spy at Watford Gap Services. I did however learn that Watford Gap is nowhere near Watford, not that one anyway.

The second thing I remember was running around

the caravan site and smashing my head on a caravan hitch. I wasn't hospitalised, but it hurt, it hurt
a lot. The third thing was that I got the job of
making sure the waste water bucket didn't over-
flow onto the grass. The contents were disgusting,
greasy, smelly washing up water and I hated it. We
only had a small bucket, in consequence it constantly needed emptying, notwithstanding the
herculean effort and trampolining caravan floor
required to fill it in the first place.

Our first summer holiday was to Scotland. This
was when we discovered that packing a caravan
for a fortnight's holiday is not a science it is an
art form. Even now, when modern caravans have
computer controlled devices and stabilisers to
prevent them waving around on the back of a car
like a demented pendulum, you have to be careful, but back then none of these things existed and
packing was indeed an art.

I guess one of the points of a family caravan holiday is economy, but that of course means you need
to take pretty much everything with you. The
task of packing was not made any easier by the
fact that the family dog was for some inexplicable
reason terrified of being forgotten. To ensure that

this could not happen she used to lie in the doorway of the van, so as you carried each load in she would be there to trip you up. You would move her and she would return to her sentry point immediately your back was turned ready to trip you up again on your way back, and so it went on with every single load.

I have spent hours in the back of a car, with my knees tucked under my chin while every little space around me was filled with the paraphernalia required to keep body and soul together when you are miles from civilisation. The caravan would be packed with clothes, sleeping bags, blankets, food, drink, water carriers, gas bottles, buckets, toys, books, outdoor games, wellies, cleaning materials for both personal and non-personal use; only for it all to be unpacked again because the nose-weight wasn't right.

Nose-weight is the downward force on the car's tow bar and you would be surprised how important it is to caravaners. Too much of it, the suspension bottoms out and the headlights illuminate the night sky as if searching for enemy bombers, not to mention the excess pressure on the suspension. Too little of it and the caravan snakes alarmingly every time it is caught in the bow wave of an overtaking lorry. I'm convinced some lorry drivers see this a sort of sport to while away the long boring hours behind the wheel, by driving as close as they can when they pass. In extreme cases caravans can turn over often taking the car with them. Eventually, after long talks between my parents, which should have been supervised by ACAS, over what it was and was not necessary to take we would eventually get everything packed. Final items went in after the human cargo had been loaded to maximise the space available. With creaks and groans the whole road train would move and we were off.

We went all the way round the coast of Scotland that year stopping at various points along the way. My dad loved driving. In my early years this was bad news for me as I suffered terribly with travel sickness. Eventually I got over it, - had to really, it was either that or, well – die! The only thing you had to keep it at bay were barley sugar boiled sweets, which tasted awful and didn't work. Frankly they used to make me feel sick even when I wasn't in a car. Scotland is a long way from Sheffield. It is with two children, one of them wanting to stop, to throw up every five minutes anyway. Gill, my wife was also a childhood caravaner and she tells me that to keep her entertained, her mum would sit in the back with her and let Gill pretend she was a hairdresser. The only problem with this arrangement was that her mother's previously, recently and perfectly coiffed hair would emerge looking something more like Jermaine Jackson's Afro on speed. This must have been truly frightening for her fellow caravaners when they arrived on site.

We spent most of our first night at a transport café at Scotch Corner on the A1 waiting for those knights of the road from the AA to tow us to somewhere where we could get the car repaired and most of the following day getting it repaired. It was so disappointing to discover that Scotch Corner is nowhere near Scotland.

My dad's sister and her family joined us for this holiday. Jan and I got on well with our cousins so we were quite happy with the arrangement. The only problem was that my dad's sister and her husband didn't really get on at all, so the entire holiday was punctuated by massive rows between them. They could fall out over anything, which way they should turn, each other's driving, packing the car, unpacking the car, what they were going to eat, putting their tent up, taking their tent down, which as we were on a touring holiday all happened frequently. Mind you in fairness I have seen many a good marriage founder on the rocks of tent and awning erection. Perhaps this is why we didn't have one.

It was a great shame that my aunt and uncle fought so much because individually they were two of the nicest people I have ever known. My uncle was one of those people whom everybody liked. Older than my parents by some years he had a hard war, including two spells as a prisoner of war held by the Italians in less than hygienic conditions and with very little food.

I can't remember when he died but he was not an old man. His was the first funeral I ever attended. I do remember, in church, a sea of turquoise and orange overalls as I think what must have been the entire workforce of the East Midlands Electricity Board, where he worked turned up to pay their respects, such was the popularity of the man.

My aunt died only fairly recently. She had a great sense of humour and when I was a child she was one of the few people who would laugh at my jokes, but only if she thought I intended to be funny. I was in touch with her for all of my life, she used to periodically travel from Chesterfield where she lived to come and spend the weekend with Gill and I on the Wirral. One of the most determined people I have ever known, she made her last journey to see us only a few months before she died just short of her ninetieth birthday.

My cousin Ian and I were about the same age - still are, come to think of it. At the time Ian was quite keen on fishing, so one day the two of us were left on the harbour wall at Oban whilst the rest of the family went and did something else. I don't suppose this would happen nowadays, but then no one saw anything wrong in leaving two ten-year-old boys, on their own, in a strange town, beside a harbour wall, with a ten foot drop to the water. What could possibly go wrong? Well Ian with his first cast caught the line in the wind which blew back and the barbed hook embedded itself in his leg. In the pre-mobile era we had no way of contacting our parents and so just had to sit there until their return. I contemplated just pulling it out, promising that it would only hurt whilst I did it and there probably wouldn't be much blood. Just as I was about to do the deed, Ian wisely changed his mind and who can blame him. Eventually, some hours later, our parents returned and took Ian to the local doctor. He went round to the hardware store, borrowed a set of pliers, snipped the barb off and withdrew the hook the same way it had gone in, leaving two neat little puncture marks. This is probably where I learnt that if you don't really know what you are doing you're probably better off leaving it to the professionals.

Other than the odd bag of chips, this was a self-catering holiday. In those days most people did not go out for dinner with their children. I didn't know restaurants even existed and had never been out to dinner at this point in my life. I cannot even remember my parents going out for a meal together until quite late in my childhood. Even then they tended to go to pubs that served food and have things like chicken in a basket rather than a full three course meal. When I talk to Gill about this she looks at me as if I was deprived and tells me that she would be made to dress in her best frock and taken to dinner at some very nice restaurants.

I did have a very kind aunt who always seemed to me to be relatively well healed. About twice a year she would take my sister and I to Sheffield and buy us some new clothes. On these occasions we were treated to lunch at a waitress service restaurant in one of the more upmarket department stores in town. I always got a headache from eating my ice cream too quickly.

Back on holiday in Scotland we nearly always had a picnic lunch of sandwiches washed down with a cup of tea. We just had standard white sliced loaves, I don't know what they made bread out of in Scotland in the 1960s but I can only hope they've changed it. The stuff was about the consistency of cotton wool and about as hard to digest. You would chew on it for what seemed like hours in the vain hope converting it into something that felt vaguely safe to swallow without choking. The only advantage was that it kept you full for hours.

Eating in a caravan was always a bit of a compromise. For one thing it was supposed to be a holiday for mum too and given that all the Lynton Scamp had was a two ring burner which doubled as a grill underneath, preparing cooked meals was always a challenge. We had a lot of Cadburys Smash. I'm not sure how nutritious it was, but we ate a lot of it. Tinned veg was also the order of the day and that took up the second ring. Meat therefore had to be something that you could grill, so there was quite a lot of grilled spam, occasionally there would be chops or sausage but remember there was no fridge so these would have to be bought and eaten on the day. By performing a juggling act with three saucepans we did have tinned stew or mincemeat and if you slopped the Smash on top of the mincemeat you could pretend it was shepherd's pie. Gill tells me that her caravan had an oven, well it would have wouldn't it? However, fridges were unheard of, even in posh caravans, so they were also reduced to anything that came in a tin. It has just struck me what a great leveller caravaning is.

Apparently her favourite was a whole tinned chicken baked in the oven. I suspect you can no longer get this. Gill's caravan apparently came with its own crockery and cutlery; all I assume bearing the Safari logo of the manufacturer. Ours was a rather more downmarket experience. We had plastic plates and plastic cutlery, all in the name of saving weight. If you stabbed your peas a little too enthusiastically the end of the fork would snap off and catapult into the air to the opposite side of the table in a neat parabola. Now if you were lucky it plopped harmlessly onto the Formica table top. If you were unlucky it went straight down the person sat opposite's clothes, or even worse, the bench seat. The resultant mess depended entirely on what you were eating at the time and was in direct proportion to the amount of trouble you were in. As the holiday progressed and the supply of spare plastic forks dwindled, there was also an increasingly detailed stewards' enquiry to determine if you should be allowed another fork.

Of course these days even entry level caravans come with gas/electric dual fuel four burner hobs, ovens, separate grills and microwaves. Added to this no self-respecting caravaner would move without a barbeque, often gas powered from a tap for the purpose on the side of the van. The strange thing is that people don't actually cook in their caravans that much anymore. We're on holiday so we go out to eat, is the attitude. I suppose it is just another measure of how the hobby has changed from being a poor man's holiday into a pastime for the affluent middle classes.

It is interesting to note that a basic caravan in 1970 was at £400 about a third of the average annual salary. It was also less than half the price of a Ford Cortina which would have set you back about £900. Today cars and caravans have rough price parity and you need approximately a year's salary to buy one. These days' caravan dealers don't even call them caravans any more. They are now leisure vehicles.

We stopped at various locations all around the Scottish coast. We visited various garages with our Ford Cortina and watched various mechanics and various AA engineers scratch their heads and proclaim the fault was electrical. I have since learnt that this is what mechanics say when they don't have a clue. Whatever it was, it was frightening to find yourself half way up some single track Scottish Highland road, in the middle of nowhere, with caravan attached when the thing would just cut out. When we did stop where we had actually planned to, we used to follow rituals, say prayers and incantations in the hope that it would start again. Even when it did start it sounded like a hyena in extreme pain. I hated that car with a passion I had not hitherto suspected I possessed. Right from its cheap sweaty plastic seats to its rusting sills and complaining engine, I hated it.

On our way home we stopped overnight at Pitlochry and that evening, after the AA man had visited, we walked up to the man-made salmon leap that was installed when they dammed the river to create a hydro-electric scheme. My sister, Jan during the holiday had been bought, at great expense, a pair of genuine Dr Scholl exercise sandals. We were stood at the top of the salmon leap watching the resting pool I'd guess about 50 feet below. I might have this wrong; things always seem so much smaller when I revisit places I went as a child. My sis was showing off a bit by dangling her foot through the bottom half of the fence. As she withdrew her foot, the sandal fell off and plummeted into the abyss below, where it landed with a satisfying splash in the salmon resting pool. It floated tauntingly, bobbing up and down in the water.

I was a horrible child, I knew she would be in big trouble and so helpfully ran off to tell my dad, in a voice dripping with glee, what had happened. I'm not proud of this you understand but to tell it any other way would be to undermine the veracity of this account. My dad duly came to the edge and I happily pointed out the soggy Scholl to him. My sis of course was, to my great satisfaction, in floods of tears. Dad went back to the caravan and returned with a couple of crab lines, we had bought earlier in the holiday and after several attempts successfully tangled the weighted line around the sandal. He then gently pulled it all the way back up. He was, my sister's hero and disappointingly forgiving of her misdemeanour.

The next day we returned home but not for long.

Prior to having a caravan, two weeks in a boarding house or hired static caravan or memorably a week in Butlin's and that would have been it for holidays. Now however the world was our oyster, or tortoise shell at any rate. We could go away for a weekend anytime the weather looked vaguely promising.

As I said earlier my dad was a branch manager for the TSB and finished work late on a Friday. In those days' banks would close at 3:00pm every day, but on Friday they reopened for an hour at 5:00pm. This was before the days of plastic cards and cash dispensers, so for people who were paid on a Friday this was the only opportunity they had to either pay in their wages, most people were paid in cash; or to get money for the weekend.

He would therefore arrive home about 7:00pm and off we would go and arrive in the Yorkshire Dales or Scarborough at some godforsaken hour of the night. Jan and I would generally be left in the car until all the setting up had been completed, whereupon we would be transferred from under a blanket in the nice warm car to a cold nylon sleeping bag in the horribly cold caravan. We would have a day out on Saturday, Sunday morning we would spend round the site and then pack up and go home. I have to confess that in my own caravanning career I got that enthusiastic on only a very few occasions, but then perhaps I always have lacked my father's ambition.

Did I miss anything by spending most summer weekends away from home? Well I suppose I never got to go to listen to much live music. I didn't get to listen to much dead music either as there was no radio in either the car or the caravan. These days of course both would have state of the art Hi-Fi systems complete with CD or music file players, and it sounds like you have an entire orchestra in the toilet compartment, well the brass section anyway, but back then only high end cars had even a basic radio. To be fair this wasn't the only challenge in my developing any musical appreciation. Sheffield like Rome is built on seven hills, now whatever other cultural claims this may give it, they were pretty effective at blocking out the old medium wave transmitters. Pre-FM, wonderful Radio 1 broadcast on 247 metres on the medium wave but not in Sheffield where it was more crackle than pop. It was the same for not so fab 208 and as for the pirate stations bobbing up and down on the high seas, forget it. I only became aware such things had existed long after their demise. I used to think that stations boasting that they broadcast to the entire nation should be made to add, except Sheffield to the end their jingles. Television wasn't a lot better, most homes had TV Ariel's lashed to masts of a size that GCHQ would have been proud of, just to receive any snowy ghosting picture at all.

When I hear people talk about the great concerts they attended and the music venues that were the haunts of their young lives I can only nod sagely, remain silent and hope that no one asks me anything. A friend of mine recently sent me a cartoon, to get the joke you had to know something about the German group Kraftwerk. I had to fess up that I didn't and my friends referred me to Google. Even then they had to tell me precisely where to look. I am in short a musical pygmy, if that is a racist slur to pygmies I apologise unreservedly now.

My wife, looks at me despairingly when I ask questions like, "Who was Robert Plant?" and my somewhat stunted musical taste means I only like things that are instantly hummable. The nearest my fourteen-year-old self got to Rock n' Roll was, that I did have a bit of a thing for Suzie Quattro. Even then I suspect this may have had more to do with the tight black leather cat suit than the music.

A CARAVAN ABROAD

My father was nothing if not ambitious. In 1970 not many people went abroad for a holiday, not from my part of Sheffield anyway, but the next year we went for our first ever holiday overseas. Initially this was planned to be Brittany, but my dad decided that if we were spending all that money on ferry fares we needed to have guaranteed good weather and so we headed for the South of France. This was quite a risky undertaking back in the day. For one thing our car was a fairly ancient, but usually reliable Austin Cambridge. Even so a round trip of nearly 2000 miles with caravan attached, in less than a fortnight was quite something. In the event it took us three days to get there and another three to get back but at least the weather was nice.

We must have been feeling especially flush that year. We arrived in Southampton for the ferry to Cherbourg early and therefore had time to have dinner at a restaurant. This was the first time in my eleven years on the planet that I had ever been to a restaurant. Seaside cafes and fish and chip shops to be sure, but never a restaurant I loved the word and couldn't stop saying it. Still do come to think of it.

The restaurant in question was the Old Oriental Berni Inn, Southampton. It was clearly a big occasion for me as I can still remember all the details some fifty years later. In those days Berni Restaurants (terrific word isn't it?) made money by offering a limited menu but at a very keen price compared to establishments serving similar quality food. There was a choice of three starters. I had melon with a maraschino cherry and a slice of orange on a cocktail stick mounted in such a way as to make the whole thing look like a Chinese junk. The melon was obviously the hull the slice of orange the sail and the maraschino perhaps a sophisticated radar system but mainly something to hold the sail on the cocktail stick. I had never had a maraschino before and to this eleven year old boy it was the most wondrous thing I had ever put in my mouth. I asked if I could have another, my mum, who had a comparatively posh upbringing explained in a hissed whisper that this wasn't how these things were done.

My main course was a rump steak, again I think there was only a choice of three and this was the first time I had ever eaten a steak. I'd heard about it of course and grew up believing that rump steak was the most expensive thing that anyone in the world could ever have to eat, so I approached my steak with a reverence normally reserved for hallowed artefacts. I enjoyed it, I honestly did. It just wasn't quite as spectacular as a maraschino cherry. Even now, if no one is looking, I still put maraschinos in my gin and tonic.

Pudding was distinctly disappointing, consisting as it did of a rather boring and rather small block of ice-cream with no garnish at all. Secretly I had been hoping for another maraschino. I was wise enough to say nothing of course and this was still, to this point, the greatest gastronomic experience of my life. In fact, I suspect there is part of me that still measures the quality of a meal by asking myself if I am enjoying it as much as the Old Oriental Southampton. You'd be surprised by how often the answer is "No".

Quite what we did with the caravan whilst we stuffed our faces I really don't know, but the ferry I remember very well perhaps because it was a bit of a thrill being up so late at night. Free Enterprise II was its name and it was painted a bilious shade of green. If you weren't feeling sick before you boarded, just one look at the colour helped you along nicely. Originally part of the Townsend Brothers ferry fleet, the company had only recently merged with Thoresen Car Ferries and clearly Free Enterprise II hadn't received the new corporate image which was "you've been Tangoed" orange and wasn't a great improvement on bilious green. Free Enterprise II was one of Townsends first purpose built ferries. Quite what they expected their fare paying passengers to travel in before that, I shudder to think. You may remember that some seventeen years later Townsend Thoresen European Car Ferries ceased to exist following the capsizing of the Herald of Free Enterprise at Zeebrugge with the tragic loss of 193 lives and many more sustaining life changing injuries.

I once read somewhere that the "Free Enterprise"

name was bit of sideswipe at Sealink, which was the only other way to cross the channel at the time. Sealink was owned by British Railways which was of course back in 1970 state owned. Townsend considered that this gave Sealink an unfair competitive advantage since it did not have to return a profit to shareholders. It seems strange now that back then so many businesses were state owned. Apart from the railways, coal mines, electricity, gas, telephones, postal services, water, waste disposal, road building and repairs, steel production, and even some car producers were all nationalised industries. Love her or loathe her Margaret Thatcher is probably one of the few prime ministers that really did leave a legacy.

I have since learned that seven hour night time crossings of the English Channel can be undertaken in a comfortable cabin with en-suite facilities. If my father was aware of this, he kept my mother and his two children blissfully ignorant of the fact. We passed the night sat bolt upright. Not that this bothered me or my sister very much but I think my mum was less comfortable. It's always possible of course that ferries didn't have cabins in 1970. Possible, but unlikely. We didn't use the on board shops apart from my dad purchasing a litre of whisky and 400 Embassy tipped cigarettes. These were the days of duty free shopping, once you had left territorial waters, and thus a considerable bargain was to be had.

The next three days were nothing like as exciting. From early morning to late afternoon our time was spent in the back of a car with the sun getting increasingly hot the further south we travelled. I always envied my sister who had this knack of being able to go to sleep in the back of a car and uncannily wake up about fifteen minutes before we arrived. Still I console myself with the fact that I saw more of the French countryside than she did. Mile after bloody mile of it. I guess that at eleven years old tree lined roads that go on for miles and miles have limited appeal. One thing I did notice was how much more willing Frenchmen were to get their willys' out in public and just pee where they fancied. In those days Englishmen would preserve their modesty by nipping behind a tree. These days of course we don't worry about it so much. Don't tell *me* that 50 years' membership of the EU hasn't changed our national character.

JOHN MOSELEY

The French did have motorways in 1970 but it was much cheaper to take the RN roads. Well I say cheaper, but in those days they had more pot holes than Raymond Blanc had pots. It seemed 'chaussée déformée' was the most ubiquitous road sign in France. On the return journey one of the leaf springs on our usually reliable Austin Cambridge broke and we spent the night in a lay-by miles from anywhere. The following morning, we flagged a car down. After two or three attempts a farmer in a Citroen Deux Cheveaux stopped and agreed to give dad a lift to the nearest town to summons help. We were rescued by a mechanic from a local garage, but not before my somewhat resentful father had parted with a considerable number of Francs. Back then cars seemed to be repairable so long as you had approximately the right part. These days you are more likely to need precisely the right part.

Of course the failed leaf spring might also have had something to do with the fact that the caravan was laden with tinned food sufficient for a fortnight's holiday for four people. Nowadays there are legal limits about how much you can load into a caravan. There might also have been back then, but if so we were untroubled by them.

We stopped twice at caravan sites on the way down. Once near Poitiers and the following night near Limoges. The first difference we noted was that French toilets were not the same as English ones. Even the ones that looked like an English loo lacked a U-bend. This meant that they fed directly into the sewer below and consequently smelt dreadful. I don't know if it's the French diet or garlic or simply glugging all that plonk but I'm really surprised they lost at Agincourt with weapons like this at their disposal. The other slightly disconcerting thing about using a loo such as this is the length of time that elapses between evacuating your bowel and hearing the resultant and distant plunk as it hits whatever it is below. You find yourself praying that there is no splash back.

My wife, Gill, you will recall also had a caravanning childhood. She probably stayed at slightly posher establishments. She explained to me one day that the loos they encountered did have U-bends, but to accommodate this you had to walk up two or three steps and mount the basin in a rather regal manner. Apparently this afforded you a view through the gap at the top of the toilet door.

Quite what view it afforded casual passers-by is mercifully not recorded.

If you give her sufficient gin and tonics Gill will also tell you about the time she and her sister washed all the breakfast pots in a urinal. In her defence she was only eight at the time and only having sisters had no idea what a urinal was for. The French signage probably didn't make it very clear either

The second type of loo encountered in mid-France at the close of the 1960s consisted of two bricks about sixty centimetres apart between which was a hole approximately ten centimetres in diameter. This was altogether more a scary proposition.

I have heard that in the last war it was not unknown for German bomber crews to drop their deadly cargo some way short of the intended target to avoid facing the deadly flack and anti-aircraft guns that defended valuable assets. This apparently explains why the Cheshire countryside South of Liverpool and Manchester is pockmarked with random craters. Well judging by the deposits on the floor surrounding this second type of French loo it appears that previous users had employed a similar technique.

The correct use of these facilities requires that you remove your lower garments completely. Merely dropping them round your ankles will not suffice when you have mount two bricks, two feet apart. Having successfully completed this manouvre you need to squat over the said ten centimetre hole and use a precision bombing technique, unpracticed by the Brits since 617 squadron took out the Eider and Mona Dams. If you miss, don't worry about it. By the state of the messy hole a foot below your sphincter it seems that the French are not very good at it either.

My dad tried to persuade me that these continental loos were actually more hygienic than English ones, because, other than your feet, you didn't, or shouldn't anyway, come into physical contact with it. This was the first time I realised that not everything that came out of my dad's mouth was necessarily the gospel, incontrovertible truth. I can probably date the time at which I changed from cooperative child into questioning teenager to this point.

More pleasantly, and as a reward for those of you who have managed to get through the last few paragraphs with your last meal still inside you, the little villages we stopped in were delightful and everything you imagine rustic French rural life should be. Old men playing boule in dusty squares, or drinking Pastis outside pavement cafes. Groups of giggling girls gossiping by huge willow trees at the side of the small river that flowed through the village. I try not to think too much about where the sewer might have ended up.

My dad went to the local store that first evening near Poitiers and bought a bottle of wine. In 1970 we didn't drink much wine in my family. A bottle of Don Cortez Spanish plonk at Christmas maybe, but that was pretty much it. Consequently, we didn't know much about wine, so we just bought one of the bottles, with stars around the neck, that was piled high by the door, which to be fair was what most of the French seemed to be buying.

The appealing thing about it was that you got a full litre, rather than a bottle, it had a plastic top, which as we had forgotten a corkscrew was a big selling point and, and this was a pretty big *and*, it cost absolute peanuts compared with what you had to pay for a bottle of wine at home. Never mind that it tasted like Algerian belly wash, or that the plastic top would regularly launch itself, Apollo like, from the bottle, powered by the continuing fermentation of the wine therein. We had arrived in France and were going to have wine with every meal, and we did. Even I at the tender age of eleven was allowed some. I have since drunk some very fine wines indeed but do you know I still love the taste of Algerian belly wash and on the rare occasion that I visit France these days I always buy some.

That warm evening we converted the table and bench seats to beds. The gas mantle hissed, lit and further warmed an already too warm caravan and mum and dad sipped whisky from tea mugs as we had also forgotten to bring any glasses. As sleep came up on us we whispered good nights, Walton's style, across the maximum of three feet that separated any of us, listened to the chirruping of the cicadas and then disaster!

My mother screamed as a grasshopper or, something that rubbed its back legs together anyway, leapt across their sleeping bag. My father launched himself in the style of a premier league goalkeeper at said insect, several times, each one ending in an abortive and sometimes painful failure. Eventually he managed to get a stray bucket over the top of it but by this time my sister and possibly myself, were all awake and screaming.

The remainder of the night passed without event, just the gentle hum of cicadas plus the one in the bucket playing the big bass drum.

The following morning brought another first. My dad and I went to the boulangerie for some bread for breakfast. The first time you eat French bread is like swimming and making love. You never forget. We bought two loaves. We shared one for breakfast before setting off on the second day of our travels. Most of the site turned out to wave us on our way. I like to think that this was because English tourists in caravans were not that common in 1970. The reality is more probably they just wanted to make sure we left after the previous evening's disturbance.

All the lunches I can remember on both the journey there and back consisted of pulling in to a layby, dropping the legs on the caravan and eating the second loaf with some cheese. Unbelievably, by today's standards this was washed down with half a glass of wine each, after which my father continued driving. You must remember that caravans did not have fridges in those days, not ours anyway, so it would not have been possible to carry milk for tea. I know, I know, even to me it sounds a pretty lame excuse, even now.

We arrived at Canet Plage on the South West French coast shortly after just such a layby lunch on the third day. We hadn't actually booked a site. I don't think it occurred to anyone that we would need to. However, this was high summer, both the French and the Spanish were in their main holiday season and consequently we spent the rest of a very hot day searching for a caravan site with a vacancy. Eventually we alighted on Camping Domino. It had a faux Hawaiian feel to it, complete with palm trees. I half expected Steve McGarrett to come bouncing out the toilet block and shout "book 'im Danno". I spent the next eight days humming the theme to Hawaii Five-O to myself.

Caravans were crammed on tooth by jowl in the manner much loved to this day by continental caravan sites. My sister and I of course were just glad to be out of the car and really could not have cared less.

When you are in a caravan without a toilet, the

site toilet block is an important, not to put too fine a point on it, vital facility. Perhaps that's why it appears I obsess about them so much. The toilet block was sort of clean-ish. It didn't come up to my mother's exacting standards of course, these things rarely did. It didn't help that the toilet cubicles were not divided in ladies and gentlemen. Everything worked on a first come first served basis. There was one English style loo complete with direct access to the sewer and, for those of you wondering, it was about a two second drop. The mathematicians among you can work out the actual depth if you like. The remainder were continental style loos. Fascinatingly people would queue for the one English style loo, eschewing the continental ones, even the French. I remember, however unreasonably, feeling slightly resentful of this.

Each of the next eight days were spent on the beach. We did squeeze a trip in to Perpignan to do some shopping, but this was always going to be a sunshine sand and sea holiday. After three solid days in the car and the prospect of three more to get home, who can blame us. In 1970 girls still wore bathing costumes on the beach, a bikini was about as daring as it got and in any case at eleven I don't think it had occurred to me that I should be interested, or maybe I was just a late developer.

The major purchase of our trip to Perpignan was a Polaroid camera that took instant colour pictures. Well instant-ish. You took a picture, a thick card shot out of the front of the camera which you slid between two sheets of aluminium, which you then placed under your armpit for two minutes – longer if it was a cold day. Bearing in mind that most of us didn't use deodorant back then, this vaguely distasteful practice was not actually the reason that Polaroid Instant Camera's never really caught on. The cameras were expensive and bulky and the films cost a fortune. Each film only took eight pictures. Even allowing for the fact that we acquired ours half way through the holiday this gave us around two pictures a day. There is no wonder the photographic record of the Moseleys' first ever venture from these shores is to say the least, a little sketchy. On reflection, that's probably a good thing. Such shots as we do have all look the same, namely a family group sat on the beach with the person behind the camera, usually my dad, missing.

A little postscript to the Polaroid Camera story. The first shop we went into, we believed the price of the camera to be about two hundred French Francs. At the time there were just over thirteen French Francs to the pound so about £15, which was a fairly significant purchase back in 1970, the equivalent of £240 today. However, the sales assistant insisted that the correct price was two thousand Francs. Whether or not she was hoping to pocket the difference I don't know but the situation became further confused by the fact that the French for a thousand "un mille" sounded like a million to our uneducated ears. Either way she had reckoned without my dad's love of a bargain, so after much English gesticulating and Gallic shrugging we exited the shop in much the same way as the whole country exited Europe many years later. This may have been the first time I realised that the English and the French did not always get on so well. However, we did manage to purchase the camera elsewhere for two hundred Francs. When it came to getting a bargain no one was quite my dad's equal.

Shopping always was an interesting linguistic experience. Later my father learned to speak French more or less fluently, however on this first trip we knew little and spoke even less. My sister and I would regularly resort to talking in a kind of Franglais reminiscent of the sitcom "Allo Allo" My father would chastise us, explaining that it would be easier for people to understand us if we simply spoke English normally but more slowly. Then one day we pulled into a petrol station, he jumped out of the car and exclaimed to the attendant in a loud voice "Fill 'er up. La top". We never let him forget it.

It seems we were not the only English family who struggled with French. Gill, tells a story about her mother going into a pet shop to purchase a new collar for the dog they had left at home, as a kind of present to take home from the holiday. The dog was a small cross bred Collie. The shop owner produced a selection of collars. "Mais non, plus grand monsieur" explained Gill's mother. The shopkeeper went in the back and produced a selection of larger collars. "Mais non, plus grand monsieur" cried Gills mother. This went on several more times before the shopkeeper with an edge of exasperation in his voice retorted in perfect English "Madam, what have you got, a bloody lion?"

"Why didn't you say you spoke English" she said equally exasperated

"I thought you wanted to practice your French" he replied.

Back at Camping Domino a French Family from near Paris had pulled on to the pitch next to us. This was the beginning of a long friendship. They had the distinctively un-French name of Bellamy and a son and daughter called Michel and Martine who were roughly the same ages as my sister and I. We all got on very well and over the years we shared family holidays together. One year Michel and Martine spent part of their school summer holidays with us in Sheffield. My sis and I got the much better end of the deal by spending some of our school holidays in Paris.

On one occasion years later all of us went to their home in Paris for dinner. Now if there is one thing the French really know how to do, it's dinner. The occasion started in the early evening and didn't finish until well gone midnight. Pierre, Michel and Martine's father was a chef by profession and he prepared food and wines fit for gods. I was a bit older by this time, with perhaps slightly more so-phisticated tastes but I didn't think of a maraschino cherry even once. This was truly amazing food preceded by aperitifs accompanied by fine wines and followed by fine calvados.

The only problem was that we had to drive back to our caravan which was on the other side of Paris. I would probably have been about fifteen by then and was allocated the task of calling out the approach to traffic lights and whether they were red or green. Other members of the family had other jobs, though I don't recall what they were. Miraculously we arrived back safely, with my father resolving never to drink and drive again, and I don't think he ever did.

That first summer at Canet Plage Michel, Martine, Jan and I spent the days playing on the beach. I was always disappointed by the fact that no matter how long I tried to soak up the sun for I remained stubbornly white and I don't just mean a naturally creamy pink Caucasian white. I mean the kind of brilliant white you would not be disappointed to see come out of a tin of Dulux. Previously I had been able to blame this on the inclement British climate, but to find after over a week in virtually unbroken sunshine that all I had to show for it were burnt red and peeling shoulders was to say the least disappointing. In school plays I was always asked to play undertakers or characters where a cadaverous appearance added to their menace. It wasn't until I was much older and discovered cycling that I acquired anything approaching a healthy complexion.

We commenced the long journey home giving ourselves three clear days to make the ferry. Of course it is one thing spending three days in a car when you have a holiday in a strange land to look forward to at the end of it, but quite another when you are going home. On the journey down we had passed a caravan site which looked positively idyllic. There was a river overhung with trees and a play area with intriguing looking ropes and pulleys joining the trees and crossing the river. The French were not that big on health and safety back then. I don't think this has changed a lot in the intervening years. It was too early to be stopping for the night so we had passed it by, whilst making a note for the return journey. This in my head would be the one highlight of the journey home.

In the event we overreached ourselves in trying to get far enough north to stop there and we arrived after dark, which counterintuitively falls surprisingly early in the southern end of France. Thus it was too late to play beside the river and Jan and I were put in the van along with my mum who prepared something to eat.

Shortly afterwards we were joined by my father who told us that no one was to venture outside for any reason whatsoever. My dad had whilst he was unhitching and levelling the caravan in the dark using a torch had idly wondered why the waste bins were mounted high in the trees, so high that you had to reach more than the height of your head to put anything in them. Then into the arc of his torch happened a group of rats. They were apparently so big that he had first mistaken them for rabbits. The following decree was issued in a manner that Boris Johnson reminded me of some fifty years later when he announced the Coronavirus lockdown, "Stay Indoors, protect the family, save lives".

Water was to be used only from the bottled water we had with us. Nothing was to be left outside and just in case we had misunderstood him first time, no one was to go outside. A bucket would be provided for essential and emergency use only. The very small bucket that usually collected the waste water under the van was pressed into service for this purpose. It must have been bad because this time we had to share our four telephone boxes not only with each other, but also one malodorous bucket. Still at least I didn't have to empty it this time. Not surprisingly the following morning we departed early and made our way ever northward back to Cherbourg and onwards home. France was a fantastic and unique experience however it was sometime before we ventured abroad again.

If I have given the impression that my father was careful with money, I should clarify. Certainly he abhorred waste and certainly he liked to get the maximum bang for his buck. However, in many ways he could be an extraordinarily generous man. He wanted his children to experience things that his own wartime childhood had never afforded him and he was ambitious for us to get the best out of life that we were capable of getting.

The son of a locomotive engine driver, he was always convinced that his Chesterfield accent had held him back, so he and my mother worked hard to make sure that their children did not speak with Sheffield accents. Jan and I were constantly corrected on our grammar, or when we dropped 'H's or used colloquial Yorkshire expressions like, "thou" instead of you, or "sen" instead of self.

In this endeavour they were largely successful. Of course as I was growing up the world was changing and having a local accent was no longer quite such a barrier as it had perhaps once been. If it were not for spellcheck you would be able to see they achieved rather less with my spelling.

We were not poor and I was well provided for throughout my childhood, although in my early years especially I remember money sometimes being short and the family finances certainly did not run to a foreign holiday every year, so in 1971 we returned to Scotland for another grand tour. This might also have been because the budget had been blown on a new caravan and this time I mean *new* caravan, which was upgraded to a Swift Danette. I think my mum inherited some money around this time and my dad received a promotion at work. In any event the "make do and mend years" appeared to be over, although this never had any noticeable effect on my father's desire to find a bargain.

The Swift was a bit of a step up from the Lynton

for one thing it was four feet longer. This may not sound a lot but when your starting point is a ten-foot caravan, that's 40% more space. If someone farted there was actually the reasonable prospect of escaping the fall out. This caravan had also had a toilet, which should have made the offence less likely in the first place, not that we were ever allowed to use it, except under the most extreme circumstances and certainly never ever, ever for a "number two."

Someone, and we never found out who, once transgressed this rule. The inquest went on for days but no one ever fessed up. Years later, long after I had grown up and had a family of my own, I would sometimes catch my father looking at me suspiciously and wonder if he was still trying to work it out. My money has always been on my sister.

This van also had a fridge, well I say a fridge, what it actually had was a cold box under the floor accessed by a trap door. The idea was that as you towed the van along the road the draught created would keep anything inside it cool. It was in fact remarkably efficient even in very warm weather. The only problem was that when you were pitched up on a site there was no draught and the cold box was just as warm as the rest of the van. If you've never been in a caravan on a hot day I should mention that the basic construction, lots of metal and lots of glass, isn't that different from a car, so as you would expect, in hot sunshine, neither is the temperature.

Anyhow we were all delighted with our luxury and brand new caravan. It even had 12 volt electrics and its own battery, so for the first time we could watch television whilst we were on holiday. The electricity also powered two fluorescent light tubes, which whistled progressively more loudly the longer we were on holiday and the more discharged the battery became.

On some sites they used to have facilities to recharge your battery. I would carry the heavy battery across the site to the charging facility holding it against my stomach and back again several hours later. Several days afterwards I would wonder why my tea-shirt had holes in the front of it. In those days the deep cycling, sealed leisure batteries we use now had not been invented and caravan batteries were really just old fashioned heavy duty car cells, so you had to remove the cell caps to charge them. As they were charging the distilled water inside would boil and splash liberal quantities of acid over the battery which I obligingly, if inadvertently wiped off on my tea-shirt on returning it to the caravan.

It was a while and about half a dozen tea shirts later before anyone figured out the problem. In the meantime, of course several implausible hypotheses, were put forward ranging from splashback off urinals, to games of hide and seek under caravans, to the effects of acid rain. To be fair I think it was this last one that eventually led to the actual cause being identified, for which I was grateful, as most of the others blamed me to a greater or lesser degree.

The second rain soaked Scottish holiday felt a bit of a damp squib, a very wet squib actually after the excitement and endless sunny days of France. My cousins were with us again, which was really good because a wet Scotland when you are twelve years old is really not that great so we at least had someone to play with. If we had any tan at all that year it was more likely due to rust. It rained. I quite like the sound of rain on a caravan roof, it has quite a soporific effect on me, but every day we would wake up to leaden skies and more often than not thick fog. I'd been told Scotland was very scenic but on the basis of this trip I had no idea whether or not this is true.

My dad's sister and her husband had bought our old caravan so they were no longer in a tent. I would love to have been a fly on the wall when they agreed a price, for when it came to getting a bargain my aunt was more than equal to my father. It is a pity they were not around by the time Brexit came along for together they would have made a formidable negotiating team. I imagine the EU would have paid us billions just to go.

We spent a good few days in Thurso. Why? I'm not sure, but whilst there we took the ferry to Orkney. The plan was to spend the night there in a cheap B&B. However unknown to us there was some kind of big festival going on and we couldn't find anywhere to stay for love nor money. Eventually the guy that ran the local garage in Kirkwall, a man called Kenny Firth took pity on this rather bedraggled looking family who had been traipsing round the town all day, in the rain, looking for a room. Kenny appeared to know everyone on the island personally and it was he who found us a room at a, very posh by our standards, hotel. By this time even my dad didn't care about the cost.

He used to tell a story about the night we stopped there. Apparently he and my mum fancied a drink after what must have been a very trying day, so my dad left the room and went in search of the hotel bar. When he got downstairs all was as silent as the grave, being very desperate for a drink by this time, he started opening doors and peering into rooms in the hope of finding a night porter. He was just about to give up, but tried one last door which was sound proofed, but he thought he heard muffled voices behind it. When he opened it, what looked like the entire population of Orkney were stood tooth by jowl in this fug filled room, laughing loudly, downing pints and scotches and having a rare old time.

When the door opened they fell silent, but when my dad walked to the bar and ordered a couple of scotches the raucous laughter started up again. This was a Sunday evening and we suspect the local licencing laws forbade the consumption of alcohol at this unseemly hour of the night and clearly the only place this side of the Pentland Firth where a drink was to be had was the Braes

Hotel Kirkwall.

By 1972 we had just about dried out but the prospect of another dousing did not appeal to any of us. So this time we were heading back across the channel for a trip down the Rhine Valley all the way to Austria. As I said my dad loved driving. His sister's family accompanied us once again and so we had Ian and Chris as company. I seem to remember they were less enthusiastic about all the travelling which was the subject of a few family fallings out along the way.

We took the ferry to Ostend on a Belgian Sealink boat. I can't remember the name of the ferry but it was named after some Belgian King or other. I can only hope his personal hygiene was of a higher standard than that of his ferry. It stank of vomit and if you used the loo you had to walk on duckboards to avoid trailing your feet through a couple of inches of – well, I don't know, but it sure didn't smell like seawater. On reflection, that might have been a good thing. It was a very rough crossing; I was ill for most of it. The only upside was that I was never seasick again after this voyage.

I liked Germany and I liked the Germans. Most of the people I met were supremely polite, helpful, had a great sense of humour, were very generous natured and their toilets were all clean, not just clean but spotlessly pristine. You could have eaten your dinner off them, even my mother thought they were clean.

This all came as something of a surprise to me. I had been raised at a time when the war was not as distant a memory as it is today. My weekly comic was something called the Valiant, which was pretty racist by today's standards particularly towards the Germans and the Japanese. One of the comic strips was called Captain Hurricane, and the stories were all of a British Army unit fighting overseas in the last war. A literal reading would have you believe that the good captain beat the combined forces of the opposing armies single handed by flying off into what was termed "a ragin' fury" whenever he lost his temper, which was often. It was littered with phrases like "Take that you piano toothed nips!" or "I'll hit that dirty fat kraut all the way back to Berlin." I'm sure it wouldn't see the light of day now but back then this was considered highly suitable reading material for impressionable eleven to fourteen year olds. Anyhow, if my trip to Germany taught me anything, it was this; don't to believe everything that you read in the papers.

As we journeyed down through the valley staying at Koblenz and in the Black Forest I found that I loved German food and wine. The wine all tasted like Blue Nun Liebfraumilch, very palatable to my uneducated palate and let's face it, what's not to like about huge sausages in multiple flavours and mountains of chips when you are thirteen years old. The ever reliable Austin Cambridge towed the caravan on through Bavaria and over a steep mountain pass into Austria, where we stayed for about a week.

All was going swimmingly, and then I went swimming. The caravan site had a swimming pool. I'm not sure if it was chlorinated as the water probably came straight off the mountain. In any event I picked up an ear infection, and this time I was hospitalised. This was the day before we were supposed to set off on the journey back. I was shipped off to the local Krankenhaus where I was to remain for the next five days. For my Mum dad and sister, this was an extension to the holiday, for me it was five days of being poked, prodded and starved, yes starved by the medics at the Krankenhaus. I've always thought the Germans had an unfortunate word for hospital.

The Krankenhaus was run by nuns. In common with most of Austria and Germany, it was scrupulously clean and the medical care was excellent. However, they seemed to be on a one institution crusade to sort out the nation's considerable obesity problem, so food was supplied in very small quantities and it was almost always healthy.

Salads, boiled potatoes, boiled fish and green vegetables were the order of the day. I shared a room with a young Austrian, who was there with a stomach ulcer. I think they put me in with him because he spoke quite good English and could therefore translate. Clearly he had a special diet, which was even more healthy and low in acid than the one I was on. The meals were bought into the ward on trays, one for him and one for me. On the rare occasion we did have meat, what I imagined to be his meal would be served with a poached egg instead.

However as soon as the nun had left he would insist that the boiled potatoes cabbage and poached egg was mine and his was the succulent if small pork steak. Yet another of life's lessons. If you don't understand what is going on, your competitors will take advantage of this.

After I was discharged from the Krankenhaus, we returned at breakneck speed, trying to catch up time as my dad was no longer supposed to be on holiday. We got back to Ostend from Austria in less than two days, which given that we were towing a caravan all the way was quite an achievement. I think my father secretly enjoyed it. Sadly, that turned out to be our last trip to Germany, though not our last trip abroad.

The following year we went back to France and joined our friends Les Bellamy in Alsace Lorraine. This was the year that Michel and Martine came to stay with us in Sheffield for a fortnight. Jan and I then went back with them to Paris for another fortnight and we then met our parents in Alsace for the family holiday which we shared with them.

At the end of this period my spoken French was actually getting pretty good. I sort of stopped thinking what I wanted to say in English and translating it, and thought to some degree in French. I can remember one night dreaming in French, which was a really weird experience the first time it happened. It is a beautiful melodic language, my knowledge isn't good enough to know if it has the same breadth of vocabulary as English does, but if ever there was a language for poetry it has to be French.

We became quite friendly with another French family on the site. The older boy was perhaps two years older than me, impossibly good looking and I saw him as competition. You see by this time I was interested in girls, very interested. However, Jean-Paul, with his two year's seniority, wavy blonde hair, blue eyes and seductive French had all the success. Of course all the girls on site were also French so the dice were loaded against me from the start.

One day he challenged me, in front of all the girls of course to swim across the lake. Now this was a good half mile and I am pretty sure that he expected me to chicken out. If he wanted some sort of revenge for Agincourt he was out of luck because there was no way I was not going to pick up this particular gauntlet. I noted with some satisfaction that Michel declined, which was probably the sensible option. Jean-Paul and I set off across the lake. I am pleased to report that we both made it. At the other side I looked him in the eye and asked if he wanted to swim back or would he prefer to walk. Much to my relief, though I didn't show it of course, he said with a slight sneer, "Walk." This exchange did not take place in front of the girls of course, but nevertheless I felt I had won some sort of moral victory.

A year or so later Jean-Paul rocked up in Sheffield. He was back-packing around the UK and my parents had unwisely given him our address and said he could stop over a couple of nights. I think it was nearly two weeks before he left and then only after my dad had more or less chucked him out.

We did have several more trips to France but as I grew older I started to want to go on holiday without my parents. I thought I'd have a better time. In this, as in many other things I was wrong. My parents had always been fairly relaxed about the freedom they gave me, so I was within reason, for example allowed, at sixteen, to drink pretty much what I wanted.

When you are with your parent's, publicans and even the police turn a blind eye to what they probably know is underage drinking. When my cousin Ian and I went on our first summer holiday together we could not get served in either pubs or off-licences and therefore spent a dry week together in a boarding house in Margate. The following year I re-joined the family for another caravan holiday in the Lake District. It rained, but at least I got a drink.

PLACES TO STAY
THINGS TO DO
PEOPLE TO MEET

In the September of 1977 I started work. I was eighteen, and had obtained three indifferent A-Levels. On this basis I decided not to go to university and started work for the now defunct British Home Stores. I'd had a Saturday job with Boots the Chemists which I enjoyed greatly. Why Boots? Well at the time I'd thought I might be smart enough to read pharmacy. My A-level results told a different story. As things turned out BHS didn't think I was that smart either and after less than a year I was on my way to start work for the Leeds Permanent Building Society.

The thing you have to understand about the Leeds for much of what follows to make sense is this. The Leeds in its heyday didn't believe in spending any money on anything that it didn't absolutely have to, this was a good old fashioned Yorkshire building society governed by good old fashioned Yorkshire thrift. My father approved heartily. This was 1978 and maybe in view of the profligacy of financial institutions that was to follow some 30 years later this was perhaps no bad thing.

Back in the seventies it was run by a bluff Yorkshireman called W. Leonard Hyde. Now for all I know W. Leonard Hyde may have been a fully paid up, card carrying member of the Temperance Society, and a devout Methodist to boot, but he looked like a man who liked a drink. Ruddy faced and barrel chested he was someone of whom I suspect most people were to a greater or lesser extent scared. I only met him the once shortly after I joined. It was in a corridor in the old Head Office in Leeds where I was introduced as a new management trainee for Sheffield branch. As a product of the comprehensive education system, he looked at me slightly disapprovingly and declared "Thou'll be one of first lads we've recruited that didn't go to Leeds Grammar School" or words to that effect. This was probably not true but I was left feeling, exactly as I was meant to feel I suspect.

Quite why he was styled W. Leonard Hyde I never knew. Perhaps he didn't much care for his first forename, but no one, except for perhaps his wife would have dreamed of calling him "Leonard" or god forbid "Len". In fact, I'm far from convinced that even his wife would have dared to be quite so familiar. This was an era in which senior managers were routinely referred to as "sir" and even one's immediate boss received the prefix Mr. As a management trainee anyone above the level of a regional manager was called "Sir". I mentioned the possibility that WLH may not have like his first name very much. If so, he was in good company. The Leeds board of directors sort of cornered the market in vaguely embarrassing names at the time. One director R.E Chadwick, like WLH, went by his second forename "Everard." Larry Grayson was at the height of his fame at the time. Although this of course Everard's parents could not reasonably have been expected to predict this.

For some reason, that was obviously important at that moment but is now lost in the sands of time, it was deemed vital that management trainees should learn the names of the senior managers and the board of directors. To this extent we were regularly formally tested on this vital aspect of our work. Many a promising management trainee's career foundered on the jagged rocks of this test. The exam paper consisted of supplying either the director's forename or surname and expecting the candidate to supply the missing information. Famously one such candidate when confronted with the surname "Armitage" neatly wrote "Shanks" after it. The correct answer would have been to pen "Geoffrey" before it. I only know this because of the assiduous attention I paid to getting these things right. It is testament to how important these things were that I can still remember the correct answer over 40 years later, when Armitage Shanks is either deep into retirement or has departed this mortal coil.

It would be unfair of me to imply that W Leonard Hyde was not a very good manager. He was ambitious, had vision and was largely responsible for growing the Leeds from a regional building society into a truly national one. Sure he liked control, liked not to spend money, hated trade unions and he didn't suffer fools gladly, but he ran the Leeds with a rod of iron, very successfully during a period in which its branch network was largely created. "Anything the Abbey can do we can do." he would boom.

One story, which maybe apocryphal, but I like to think that it's true; is that one day he rang a branch at around mid-day and waited a rather long time for someone to pick up the phone. When they eventually did, he bellowed at the unfortunate clerk "Do you know how long it took you to answer this phone?"

"No I'm sorry I've just got back from having my haircut" the clerk replied

"In the company's time?" shouted W Leonard Hyde. "Do you know who I am?"

"No" replied the clerk. "Do you know who I am?" he continued pensively

"NO!" shouted the by now apoplectic W Leonard Hyde.

"Phew thank goodness for that." Said the clerk and put the phone down.

As I say it may not be true, but it jolly well ought to be, if only because it perfectly illustrates the fear and awe in which the great man was held.

A final idiosyncrasy of the great WLH was that

he could not bear to see a man with a beard, to be fair the same probably went for women too. I think he took the view that this made a man look officious or unfriendly and this was not the image he wanted The Leeds to portray. However if you wanted to pop a few nails in the coffin of your career, joining a trade union and growing a beard would have done the job nicely. He wasn't on his own another manager I knew refused to employ anyone with a beard. "If a blokes too lazy to shave he's too lazy to work" was his view. No amount of informing him of all the hairy high achievers that had gone before; Darwin, Shakespeare, Lincoln, Stalin Billy Connolly etc. would shift it.

His wish for control meant the Leeds in those days was a very much centralised organisation. All the final lending decisions were taken in the head office in Leeds. Branches although free to decline mortgage applications were not able to approve them. They were largely post boxes for head office and places for the public to deposit and withdraw cash. Younger readers may be interested to know that cash dispensers were in their infancy in 1978 and unheard of at the Leeds.

I opened by mentioning the Leeds love of parsimony. By way of illustration allow me to relate something that happened in my first year.

I was "encouraged", by my branch manager, quite forcefully as I remember to attend and get involved with the local Building Societies Institute (BSI). Never having been one who functions especially well in a large group, I was reluctant, but it was made clear to me that this was nearly as important as learning the names of the directors and so I acquiesced. The real reason my cooperation was required, was that the various building societies in Sheffield competed for tickets to the Annual Building Societies Institute dinner. A black tie only event to which branch managers invited their best business contacts as a reward. Nowadays such invitations would be declined for fear of bribery allegations, but it was different back then. The more tickets a branch manager could obtain the more bankers and solicitors he could invite to this prestigious event. In Sheffield tickets were allocated based on how well each society supported the local Building Societies Institute throughout the year, hence the three-line whip to get involved.

In those days a large part of a branch manager's

job was to entertain the local banking and legal fraternities in the hope of persuading them to get their wealthier clients to invest their money with the society. With an insatiable demand for mortgages building societies were desperate for deposits and anyway what else was a Manager to do with their time, it wasn't as if they had to spend hours approving loan applications. So I dutifully attended all the meetings and became secretary for the local BSI organising committee.

My role as secretary was to record the minutes, type them up and post copies to each committee member after each meeting. Most of the committee members also worked in building society branches in the city and could be delivered by hand. However, there were always three or four copies that needed to be posted to the further outreaches of South Yorkshire.

Now Sheffield was quite a big branch, with a lot of post, but no franking machine. This was deemed an expensive and unnecessary luxury, so each individual letter sent was duly recorded in a post book with a note as to whether it was first or second class, usually second, and the cost of the postage entered. Thus there was no way to smuggle my three or four letters through this impressively secure system. Anyway the lady that controlled the post book did not like me and would have grassed me up immediately. I doubt even knowing the first and last names of the board of directors would have saved me.

I don't think her dislike was personal. However unfairly, in those days men were recruited as management trainees and thus had a career path. Women were recruited as shorthand typist/cashiers which they were expected to remain. She, not reasonably, resented this.

I went cap in hand to my branch manager's office, knelt before him and asked if I might include the copies of minutes that absolutely needed to be posted in the branch post. He sucked his breath in through his teeth and muttered something about it being "highly irregular." I countered that I was only in this position because he had asked me to "get involved with the BSI" but if he would prefer I would present the BSI with a bill for four postage stamps each month? This had the desired effect. I think he could see all those extra BSI Annual Dinner tickets flying to the competitors' arms at the Nationwide or wherever. He told me to leave it with him.

I heard nothing for about a week. Then I received a phone call from one of the four Assistant General Managers of the society a Mr Germane. Edward Spencer if you are interested – see, it never leaves you. Now Edward Spencer Germane was highly irregular himself. For one thing he liked to be known as "Ted" by everyone from the cleaners upwards. No "sir" handle for this guy, Self-styled champion of the workers he was universally popular, among the proletariat anyway. Even so an AGM phoning me? I took the receiver with some trepidation. I think he probably understood the impact his call might have. He was friendly to a fault, asked me how I was getting on and had obviously taken the trouble to find out a couple of snippets about me. He told me of course it was OK to use a bit of postage to support the BSI and if anyone had a problem with it, to refer them to him. After a few more pleasantries our call ended.

I rather inadvisably told my branch manager about the call. It did not go down well, but I was only eighteen. With a few more years on my back I might just have omitted the name dropping. Interesting though, that a General Manager was required to approve expenditure of around £2 a month in today's money. As I say the Leeds in its heyday didn't believe in spending anything that it didn't have to.

Of course starting work did limit my caravanning career, although I did periodically still join my parents. However, they had by now exchanged the caravan in favour of a motorhome, so if I did go with them I had to stay in a pup, tent or the awning. They had quite a posh motorhome, a Mercedes no less. Even so, I'm not sure they ever totally got on with it as some years later they reverted back to a caravan. I guess motorhomes do have advantages, they are easier to drive, and there isn't as much work to do when you arrive on site. However, they drink fuel and if you get all set up and then discover you have forgotten say the milk, you have to put everything away again just to drive off and get it, as the motorhome also doubles as your car. Some people get around this by towing a small car behind the motorhome, but that seems to me to defeat one of the major advantages of getting a motorhome in the first place.

Just over a year after I started at the Leeds I met my wife - in a car crash! Actually I engineered it, the meeting that is, not the car crash. Gill lived not far from me and I had admired her from afar for a while however we did not move in the same circles and I never seemed to manage to meet her in a situation where we could have a conversation that went beyond a nod or a smile.

We both worked in Sheffield City Centre and we would finish work at approximately the same time. I did not normally take my rather ancient Mini to work as it was much cheaper to take the bus, but this time I wanted to impress, with my twelve-year-old Mini Clubman.

I timed my run to the bus stop, by her place of work, to perfection. I opened the door and casually asked if she would like a lift home. Gill, who probably didn't believe this was an entirely chance encounter, lived a couple of doors up the road from me and probably, unable to see a way out of it, accepted.

On the way home we were involved in an accident. In fairness I had stopped at a red light and the driver behind didn't. No one was hurt, but after exchanging details we continued on our way with quite a dent in the rear end of the car and quite a dent in my confidence and pride. Still, she did agree to go out with me. We got married just over two years later and the rest as they say is history.

Gill's family had also had a caravan in which she had taken most of her childhood holidays and whilst it would be many years before we could afford one ourselves, at least I was now married to someone who understood. It should be noted that her caravanning experience was slightly more up-market than mine. For one thing they towed with a three litre Ford Capri, a very desirable car back in the day and they had a very upmarket Safari caravan to match. It was not until 1989 that Gill and I got our first van. The technology had moved on significantly since the seventies.

Gone were the trampolining manual foot-pumps. Water was now pumped by an electric pump. Out, were the glass windows that used to drip with condensation. These were replaced with plastic double glazed units making the caravan much warmer. They came complete with roller blinds and fly screens so in the summer you could sleep with windows open. The bucket had been re-placed by a flushing loo which was emptied by re-moving a cassette on the outside of the van. No more sharing your living space with the recent contents of your bowl.

You now plugged caravans into mains electricity, they had central heating, hot and cold running water, showers, four burner hobs and ovens, refrigerators with freezer compartments, all of which could be powered either by mains electricity or bottled gas. No more liquid butter and solid milk. You could even make ice to put in your gin and tonic along with a maraschino.

Yes, caravanning had undergone something of a revolution in our ten-year absence. The price of caravans had also undergone something of a revolution. We paid just over £6000 for our first caravan in 1989 that's around £16,000 in today's money and that was after visits to several dealerships in search of a bargain. In my experience there are two types of caravan dealer. There are the ones who will give you a big price and allow you to haggle them down and the ones who will simply quote you a lower price but refuse to negotiate. The latter are to be preferred.

Gill said we needed an awning, I declared loftily, no we don't. I explained that my family had managed without an awning perfectly adequately for many years both at home and abroad. We went away for one weekend, just two nights and we got an awning. By this time, we had a six-year old daughter and a two-year old son and Gill was of course, as usual, right. Awnings do however have some disadvantages.

One Easter we went to Anglesey when there was a huge storm. Half-way through the night we heard the awning start to pull away from its anchor points. I jumped up pulled a pair of wellies on, picked up a mallet and ran outside to hammer the canvas back down. I reasoned that at three o'clock in the morning no one would see me so I didn't worry about my attire or rather lack of it. I was just attaching some extra guy ropes when I noticed that our neighbours were all out making the same emergency repairs as myself. However, they had all had the foresight to wear a little more than underpants and wellies.

Our first weekend away was to Much Wenlock in Shropshire. It was almost as wet as Scotland. We spent a big chunk of the weekend in the van playing with the children trying to keep them amused and we loved it.

We arrived much too late on the Friday night to get onto the site and so pitched on the late arrivals area, moving on to the site on the Saturday morning. Thus another big chunk of time was spent pitching, hitching, unhitching and pitching, again all in the rain. Still we got very good at it. I appreciate that to the uninitiated this doesn't sound much but it's not quite as straightforward as it seems. There is the art of getting the van into approximately the right position in the first place. As fellow caravaners will know this provides hours of endless entertainment on caravan sites, especially when a novice arrives and I don't know what it is, but you can usually tell.

I have known touts sell prime position seats and provide glasses of wine at extortionate prices for the complete, never-to be-forgotten day out, experience. Even after all these years I am not particularly great at reversing a caravan. I have seen people who are and I can only watch and admire in envy. It is however a far, far superior event if you get to watch someone who is completely useless at it. Even better if husband and wife have a blazing row over whether it's the driver's fault or that of the person giving directions. I have watched some truly memorable fights over this important matter. These days many caravans have motor movers which turn them into giant remote control toys and this takes all the fun out of it.

Motor movers are a relatively recent invention. They apply a roller to each of the road wheels which is powered from the caravan battery. The operator has a cordless remote control with directional buttons on it thus allowing them to move the van in any direction with pinpoint accuracy. This is especially useful when connecting the caravan to the car. For older caravaners, without hunky children to do the heavy pushing and pulling, a motor mover is essential. So if you do see someone pitching a caravan manually and badly these days you are fortunate indeed. It is the caravanning equivalent of spotting a kingfisher.

Once you have got the thing pitched it needs unhitching. Clearly it's more than a piece of rope that joins car and caravan together. There is a coupling head with a locking mechanism. There are either one or two electric cables, depending on design, to keep all those mod cons you carry powered up. There is a safety chain, which applies the brakes in the event of a sudden, unplanned and dismaying decoupling along the road. The coupling head is usually fitted with a stabiliser device to restrict the caravan hitch movement around the tow ball thus making the caravan obedient to the cars wishes rather than the other way round. A jockey wheel to help with levelling and stop the front end hitting the deck. Oh and don't forget to apply the manual brake, especially if you are doing all this on a slope, otherwise you risk your pride and joy slipping majestically backward in the manner of a newly launched ship with a potentially less elegant finish over the edge of a cliff, or into somebody else's caravan.

Unless you want to roll out of bed all night you have to level it both fore and aft and side to side. The latter is the trickier, hence most caravaners carry a veritable forest of planks and assorted blocks of wood around in their boots to pop under the wheels. This last task has gotten even more challenging in recent years as modern security wheel clamps require the wheel to stop in precise alignment with a receiver, otherwise they won't fit. Many is the time I have set everything up only to discover that I can't get the wheel clamp on. Once you have one all this you can drop the corner steadies, apply all your security devices and connect up the services – water, electricity and drainage. So there is quite a lot of stuff to get good at, and sometimes you need to do all this with it raining horizontally at you. To enjoy caravanning you really do have to enjoy the hassle.

As with all hobbies it is not entirely unknown for a fellow caravaner to share the benefit of their much greater knowledge and experience with you by shouting helpful advice like "You're doing it all wrong."- From a safe distance of. However, like everything else once you have done it a few times it all becomes second nature and then you can tell everyone else that they are doing it all wrong. If you do take this approach, don't come complaining to me when someone unplugs you from the electricity, when they pull off the following morning.

In this country there are broadly three types of caravan site. Firstly there are the club sites operated by the Caravan & Motorhome Club and the Camping & Caravan Club. Incidentally these organisations started off being called The Caravan Club and the Camping Club respectively, which I suppose shows how the hobby has changed over the years.

Club sites are in many people's eyes the epitome

of luxury caravanning. To say you are staying on a club site is the caravanning equivalent of letting it slip that you have a flat in Mayfair or Belgravia. They usually offer top end facilities, such that you would not be disappointed to find in a luxury hotel and if you really want to keep up with the Jones's then these days you can get a super-pitch which will allow you to connect to mains water and drainage along with mains electricity and satellite television.

They don't normally have bars and clubs on them, which would be considered vulgar by some of the caravanning fraternity's elite. They do normally have lots of signs warning you to keep off the grass, pitch in line with pitch markers. Still others warning of the dire consequences of washing clothes in the showers, or your pots in sinks designated for laundry and many other potential transgressions. I exaggerate, but the Caravan and Motorhome Club especially used to have a vaguely military feel to it and even now they do like things done in the right way. Members receive a magazine each month full of interesting stuff, well interesting to us caravaners anyway. The letters page is an usually entertaining. There's normally something from Disgusted of Tunbridge Wells along the lines of "someone pulled their wheeled water container across the grass in front of my caravan in the early morning dew, leaving clearly visible tramlines." Not a club member. Surely?

Many years ago we pitched up at a club site in East Yorkshire where I was fairly officiously told I didn't have a booking. After standing to attention for a full five minute dressing down I was informed that my booking was for the previous week and I hadn't turned up, He didn't quite call me an "orrible little man" but that was the tone of the discussion.

I'm not sure whether the slip up was mine or theirs, However, I thought better of insinuating the latter and instead bravely asked if we could stay anyway. The site which probably took a 150 caravans was virtually empty. Even so I was only grudgingly admitted, and subjected to withering looks throughout my stay. To be fair this was very much the exception and it would never happen today. All of the site wardens that I have come across in recent years are friendly, welcoming, have a great sense of humour and will go out of their way to help you.

The second type of site are the large commercial ones. These often cater both for static caravans and tourers. They are holiday parks in themselves sometimes providing night clubs, pubs, restaurants, slot machine arcades, swimming pools and children's play areas. The cost of a night's stay can be eye-wateringly expensive and they can be quite crowded. Therefore, such establishments are generally eschewed by the Moseley family. Space is money and on some such sites therefore you don't get a lot of it.

Some years ago I was working in Milton Keynes at a time when my employer was a bit short of readies. It was the week before I was going on holiday, so I said I would stop in my caravan, instead of an hotel, if they would pay my site fees. They gleefully rubbed their little hands together and I gleefully rubbed mine. This was November time. Many sites close at the end of October so my only option was a large commercial site of the type I describe above. No matter, at this time of year I had the enormous field set aside for tourers to myself for the whole week. Gill caught the train and joined me on the Friday. All week I had been telling her how empty the site was.

Unfortunately, not being very observant, I had failed to spot that this was the weekend that this particular site chose to hold its bonfire and firework extravaganza. I picked Gill up at the railway station on Friday evening and drove back to the site I had left empty that morning to find it packed so tightly you couldn't even open the caravan door fully. Our neighbour, a particularly frightening looking woman of a certain age, with bottled blonde hair, dressed in a leopard print dressing gown, swigging gin from a bottle, was applying her slap, with liberal abandon, using our caravan window as a mirror. She eyed us both suspiciously as we approached. Gill arched an eyebrow at me. "I'm in trouble here" I thought. Not the sort of trouble you get out of with a bunch of flowers and a couple theatre tickets, real trouble, and I was.

We left early the following morning after a sleepless night punctuated at intervals by sounds of loud music, drunken voices, breaking glass and cries of ecstasy, from those, for whom if the earth didn't move, the caravan certainly shifted a bit. All personal choice of course but that dear reader is why we don't use some commercial sites very much.

It would be wrong of me to infer that this is a typical description of all commercial sites. There are many others which aspire to a much more tranquil atmosphere. Many are indistinguishable from club sites and provide excellent facilities. They do however tend to be larger establishments and our favoured choice is something much smaller.

The third type of caravan site you will find in the UK is the Certificated Location or CL for short. Prior to 1960 there was nothing in legislation to stop you pitching your caravan just about anywhere. The landowner might get a bit upset about it, but pitch in a layby say and there wasn't much anyone could do about it. Legislation that year made wild camping illegal in most places, but part of the legislation dealt with the establishment of Certificated Locations.

This allowed qualifying organisations, which means the two caravanning clubs, to issue certificates allowing say, a farm or pub for example to accommodate up to five caravans without the need for planning permission or a licence. There are now several thousand such sites in the UK. They vary from the very basic, a tap and somewhere for waste-water and sewage, to those providing electric hook-ups and toilet blocks that would be quite at home on some full facility club sites. A few even have super-pitches. They are usually cheaper than large sites and therefore, you've guessed it, much favoured by the writer.

Of course you don't always get billiard table like green lawns to pitch on and I've spent some nights with my caravan at a precarious angle where ropes would have come in handy just to get into and stay in bed. I've also needed to be hauled on and off the pitch by the local farmer's tractor on more than one occasion, but there are some very beautiful and peaceful places to stay.

Out of the main season you will often have the whole place to yourself. Some are located at country pubs, so you can eat and drink what you like, wave at the local bobby waiting outside for potential drink drivers, safe in the knowledge that you only have to stagger across the car park to your caravan and close the door. The local bobby of course thinks you are heading for a car and at the last minute you disappoint them. I really love doing that.

There are some very interesting CLs indeed. Just

outside Stonham Aspel in Suffolk there is a site
set in an orchard where the farmhouse has a wide
moat all the way round it. There is a land bridge
of course but the loo and shower are attached to
the farmhouse. One evening Gill went to use the
facilities and in the dark was unable to locate the
bridge to find the secret of the way back. Eventually I went to look for her and I did find her
marching up and down the house side of the moat
with a perplexed expression on her face. "You
could always swim" I shouted helpfully. Her reply
is unprintable.

The evidence seems to be that CLs are getting
fewer in number. Every month in the Caravan and
Motorhome club magazine there are lists of newly
opened CLs and closures. The latter always seems
to be significantly longer. Through regular use,
we have got to know some CL owners very well
indeed. The CL in Suffolk is a nine-hundred-acre
arable farm where the farmer taught me quite a lot
about how you market cereal crops. It's a lot more
complex than you might think. A failed American
harvest of soya beans has huge positive implica-
tions for the price of rape, which is used as a sub-
stitute. A barley crop that is good enough to go

for malting is worth a lot more money than one which is only good enough for animal feed.

Farmers will sell some of their crop into co-operatives where they can get a guaranteed, if not the highest price. They will create futures backed by a proportion of their expected crop. For many years one of the more complex subjects I used to teach financial advisers was about the use of futures and options employed by derivative traders and fund managers. Little did I realise that farmers create such instruments as a way of protecting themselves against sudden movements in world prices. Being a farmer isn't all about sitting on a tractor and my Suffolk farmer understood complex financial instruments far better than I did.

Another Shropshire farmer taught me all I know about guns. Unfortunately, one day he took one to his wife, ended up in prison and that was another CL on the closure list.

In North Shropshire, less than forty miles from home is the place where we do most of our winter caravanning. Whitchurch is probably not most people's idea of a primary holiday destination but when all you have is a weekend and you don't want to travel far there is actually quite a lot to do round here. We have visited so often, that we have almost become part of the community. We go to friends' houses for dinner and they come to the caravan in return. The local pub and Indian takeaway view us as regular customers. In the countryside people are a little more dependent on their neighbours, so you tend to get to know them better even though they may live a quarter mile up the road. Walking the dog takes me forever by the time I have stopped and chatted with the friends I meet. It always strikes me as strange that I probably know the neighbours better by this CL than I do those at home where they are just over the garden fence.

When we had young children we stayed on many club sites and on some commercial ones. As they got older we tended to use more CLs and now it is just Gill and I we are more or less exclusive CL caravaners.

Our first trip abroad as a family took place in the summer of 1990. Tom was about three and Phillipa would have been coming up to seven. It was to Alsace Lorraine on the border between France and Germany. We landed at Boulogne and being a bit of a chip off the old block I didn't want to use the motorways, for which you had to pay a toll. The only problem was that finding a way out of Boulogne that wasn't on the motorway didn't seem to exist. Believe me, I spent an hour driving round the town trying. I drove past the same gnarled, cigarette smoking, not to mention nonplussed Frenchman half a dozen times. On the final fly past he did his bit for the entente cordial by waving to us. That was the last straw for Gill and so I had to concede defeat and open my wallet. As you can tell it's taken me some getting over.

Although caravans had advanced considerably in the intervening ten years, French plumbing had not, as was confirmed by our first stop at a service area. I say service area, but as many of you will know there are not actually any services at most French motorway service areas. I had read somewhere that if you drive barefoot you will get greater fuel economy. It is a mark of my gullibility that I tried this all the way down to Alsace. All I got was very dirty feet. If I look hard enough I suspect some of the grime from this ill-advised experiment is still there. I have also since read that it is quite dangerous. Barefoot is also not the best way to enter a public toilet, whatever country you are in, but especially France.

Not quite having my dad's spirit of adventure I did pre-book a site at which we arrived safely on the second day. The other thing that had not changed was the continental ideal of cramming as many caravans as possible into the smallest possible space. To be fair this was an especially hot summer and everyone was trying to pitch under the one little copse of trees available on site. So most of the more exposed pitches were completely empty. The whole effect was that of a Bedouin tribe taking over an oasis in the desert.

At the bottom of the site behind the desert there was a freshwater spring. The water came out the ground at a constant cool temperature and supplied all our drinking water that year. It had been dammed so there was a pool in which you could store your beer, white wine and soft drinks. Of course everyone on the site used it, so the pool looked like a kind of underwater off licence. Everyone respected ownership, even of some quite expensive bottles of Champagne. One thing about caravaners is that they are a pretty honest lot. If you think about it, by the time you take account of submersible water pump, water containers, toilet chemicals, steps, chairs, tables, barbeque, you leave several hundred pounds' worth of easily portable kit outside the van and none of it ever disappears.

We had some very hot days, and after one particularly arduous mountain walk we arrived back in the village by the site and Gill understandably said she didn't want to cook. She was wearing an off the shoulder sundress and I was wearing a pair of shorts. Just a pair of shorts, I hadn't taken a shirt with me and the children had swimming costumes on. We were all looking slightly grubby after a day's walking. This would be about 5:30 in the evening, so we agreed we would have something to eat on the terrace of what appeared to be a café. The French waiter looked at his watch when we asked for a dinner menu. Any self-respecting Frenchman would not dream of ordering dinner any time before 8pm, however he reluctantly took our order with a slight sneer, padded off towards the kitchen and we waited. We waited some more and having finished our pre-dinner drinks we ordered a bottle of wine and waited some more.

At around 7:00 our starters arrived, we gobbled

them down in hungrily, as if we hadn't eaten for a week, much to the barely disguised disgust of our waiter. We ordered more wine and waited some more. By now the children were getting restless and we were getting drunk. The French were starting to arrive for dinner at the café which as evening had drawn on had now magically transmogrified from corner café into a nice restaurant. They were dressed in all their chic Parisian finery, as befits an evening out in convivial company.

Of course what they got was this squiffy, bare torsoed, English couple with their dirty, unruly children. Our main courses arrived which we ate hurriedly between hissed admonishments to the children in all too loud a whispers. We paid the bill and made an ignominious exit. I think we may have set Anglo-French relationships back a couple of years that evening. There were only two restaurants in the village and so far as we were concerned there was now only the one. We did visit this alternative restaurant several times and very nice it was too, but we always felt we had to be on our best behaviour.

That was our first trip abroad as a family but we did go many more times visiting Belgium, Luxembourg Germany and The Netherlands, of which much more later.

One of the guaranteed ways to do your bit for international relations on a foriegn caravan site is to start a game of French cricket. Despite its name, the French do not have a clue what you are doing. Phillipa, Tom and I would go out on to the children's' play area armed only with a cricket bat and tennis ball; you don't need a lot of kit for French cricket. Within half an hour you would have upwards of twenty kids of various nationalities all playing. The rules don't need any explaining, most people pick them up simply by watching for a few minutes so language isn't a problem.

The real beauty of this is that once you've got the game going you can retire to a sun lounger with a beer, nobody notices and you get all the credit for entertaining not only your own, but everyone else's children.

As the Phillipa and Tom grew up of course we had to do some of the more sophisticated holidays. At fifty-five quid a night in the mid-nineties, Camp Davy Crocket at Euro-Disney remains the most expensive caravan site we ever stopped on. Mind you we did have an absolutely fantastic time.

The weather was hot the whole time and the entertainment endless from the early morning trips up the travellators to the main entrance to Disneyland, to the evening's electrical parade. Early mornings, long days and late nights.

On one occasion my daughter Phillipa, who would have been around ten at the time was so exhausted with the heat that she became faint and burst into tears. A child is not allowed to cry in Disney. True to their word Mickey and assorted Disney characters appeared from nowhere and spirited us off, magic carpet-like to a first aid post. I'm not kidding, you could have carried out open heart surgery in this place. In the event a couple of glasses of water were all it took before we were on our way.

So much did we enjoy our stay, that on the day we were coming home, we spent the morning in the swimming pool trying to delay our departure for as long as possible. It's a fantastic swimming pool, complete with wave machine and water rapids to swim through. We should have left about two hours sooner than we actually did, thus we had a very high speed dash back to Calais. I nearly didn't have time to get any Algerian belly wash, but we did make it and we even picked up some wine along the way. A final plug for Euro-Disney; there isn't a continental style toilet to be seen anywhere in in the place or on the campsite. The loos are so clean that Gill could have washed her pots in them. God bless America.

As the years passed we began to struggle to know quite what to do with holidays. There is a three and a half year gap between our children. That was quite awkward to manage and you can't play French cricket all the time. What the younger one wanted to do bored the other and what the older one wanted to do the younger was too small for. That conundrum was what lead to the next phase of our caravanning adventure.

NORTH SEA CROSSING

Nobody spoke, not even my normally vocal, never fail to voice an opinion, thirteen-year-old daughter. All four of us gaped terrified at the Everest style slope in front of us that we now had to pilot car and caravan up, laden with four bikes on the roof rack and supplies for an economic fortnight's holiday in Europe.

If we were ever to get this adventure further than the east most end of the M62 however, we now had to board the ferry. The slope in question was the vehicular entrance to P&O North Sea Ferries flagship, Norsea, since renamed Pride of York and the reason for our collective silent hysteria was something that had happened earlier that year. That year being 1995.

At the time I was lucky enough to qualify for a company car. The choice was dependent on your grade and given that we had a caravan I had always hitherto chosen the biggest car my employer was prepared to pay for. Not being very senior this meant not very big cars so I had a succession of Ford Sierras and Mondeos. Now great car though the Mondeo is by 1995 I was pretty bored with them. The name Rover still had a little kudos attached to it in those days and vainly I really, really wanted a Rover. The problem was that the only one I could have was the Rover 400. Significantly less powerful and smaller than the Mondeo. I really should have known better, swallowed my pride and had yet another Mondeo, but I didn't and sure enough on a holiday to the Peak District, we got stuck halfway up a hill somewhere between Stoke on Trent and Ashbourne.

We had just come round a tight bend, the car looked at the gradient in front and decided, "No" It simply stopped. I chucked everyone out of the car and tried to restart on the hill with the family vainly and probably dangerously pushing at the back of the caravan. I tried reversing slightly so that the van was at a slight angle thus making the take up of the weight a little more gradual when I went forward but there was no way it was going to move.

We were lucky that day, after fifteen minutes of head scratching a Good Samaritan happened by. He was coming in the opposite direction, down the hill and stopped to enquire if we were OK. I explained our predicament. He asked if I had a tow rope, which as luck would have it I had just acquired that very morning. Using the tow rope to lash his car to mine we double-headed the caravan to the top of the hill. Gill and the children had to run along behind and arrived some minutes later red-faced, out of breath and not very happy with me, but nonetheless relieved. It is easy to be cynical about what can seem to be an increasingly selfish world, but do you know something, when it comes to the crunch most people are really kind and will try and help you if they can.

By some judicious route planning the rest of the holiday passed without incident and I vowed never to go anywhere with hills ever again or at least until I had changed my car. Our summer holiday was going to be in the Netherlands. Can't get less hills than that I reasoned so it was with absolute confidence that we set off for Hull to catch the overnight ferry to Rotterdam. That was before we saw the entrance to the car deck.

In those days' cars were loaded first on to a hoistable car deck which was duly hoisted and the remaining cars went underneath. Caravans went up the steep slope and were squeezed between the hull and the the now hoisted car deck. I guess you had around eight inches' clearance either side between the hull of the ship and the car deck, so it was at the best of times a delicate manoeuvre. I had watched several caravans in front of me go slowly over the substantial speedbump positioned where the stern ramp met the harbour wall, climb gingerly up the steep slope and carefully disappear down the side of the narrow passage at the side of the car deck and now it was my turn. The Derbyshire hills came unbidden into my mind. The fear and shame of being stuck half way up that damn ramp weighed heavily on my mind. I also had the not entirely irrational belief that the only way I was going to make it was to take a run at it.

I took a deep breath, popped the clutch and with the engine screaming for mercy bounced over the speed bump with the four bikes on roof rattling alarmingly. I floored the accelerator and we shot up the slope. As the car hurtled over the summit I stood on the brakes and screeched to a halt behind the caravan that had preceded me with inches to spare. A cloud of smoke and lethal asbestos dust billowed out from the wheel arches. I looked in the wing mirror to check I had not hit the hoistable car deck, just in time to see a loadmaster in his high visibility jacket pointing his finger at the side of his head.

Now I don't profess to have any skill with lip reading but the first word certainly began with an "F" and I'm pretty sure the last one was "Idiot". I couldn't even disagree with him. I tried not to think about the return journey for the next two weeks. When I did, I reasoned that we would have eaten the food we were carrying and the whole rig would be lighter. Desperation makes you clutch at such straws. In the event we managed the return journey without a hitch or indeed the same histri-onics.

This wasn't our first visit to the Netherlands but it was the first time we had used the long sea crossing rather than driving down to Dover and then across France and Belgium to reach our destination. The design of the short sea crossing roll on roll off ferries is significantly different to that of the North Sea Ferries which are more akin to small cruise ships, but I really hadn't understood the near catastrophic difference this would make to what should be the relatively simple process of boarding a ferry.

It wasn't even our most disastrous sea crossing. That honour goes to one we made from Suffolk the year before and it was all my fault again. At the time, I wasn't that flush so I had been looking for the cheapest possible crossing and boy did I find it. The "no frills" banner more than lived up to its name. The crossing was on a cargo ferry and I still cringe when I think of the dismay on my family's faces as they surveyed the rust bucket I had placed faith in to get us across the North Sea.

"I've heard that the North Sea is one of the shallowest seas in the world." I said reassuringly. It didn't work.

"You've been saving money again haven't you?" they shouted accusingly.

Amid threats to make sure there was no space on

any lifeboat for me in the very likely event of my needing one and threats to phone ChildLine in the very unlikely event that we made it across to the other side, they eventually agreed to board.

Now until this point we had experienced only nice, clean ferries that had shops, restaurants, bars, children's play areas, our own cabin, complete with shower and nice people to travel with. This one had just a single room about the size of half a badminton court. It was filled with non-matching Formica topped tables with tubular steel legs and non-matching hard chairs made of similar materials in various stages of disrepair. We shared this space with a number of mostly East European, beer bellied, unshaven lorry drivers, who belched and farted at regular intervals. They regarded us suspiciously and made what I imagined to be lewd comments to each other about the only two females in the room which just happened to be my wife and daughter.

The final straw came when one of them set up an ancient television and VHS video player on one of the tables and proceeded to show a porn movie. We spent the remainder of the voyage on the outside deck freezing and I at least enduring cold sullen stares. I hope that over the years I have created some wonderful memories for my children, however this is the one they frequently choose to remind me of. I should consider myself lucky I wasn't made to walk the plank.

To return to the rather more upmarket P&O North Sea Ferries flagship though, after the trauma of boarding we did have a bit of a treat. I was obviously still feeling the need to make amends, but cheaply. Some months earlier I had written to P&O and asked them if we might visit the bridge of the ship. They wrote a carefully worded letter back to me explaining all the reasons why this would in all probability not be possible, but if I presented this letter at the reception desk they would see what they could do. Once we were on board this was the first thing I did, a very helpful steward made a telephone call and an officer arrived who took us all up to the bridge explaining that now was the best time as we could watch the ship leave port.

It was like the bridge of the Starship Enterprise up there. In those days the Norsea had to be maneuvered from its birth through a giant sea-lock and lowered to the level of the River Humber below.

The ship had been built to fit the lock so there was no more than two feet clearance on either side. The officer explained to us this wasn't a problem as the ship had been designed to sail sideways if necessary. I had been hoping for a huge ships wheel such as one might see on a pirate's galleon. It was a tad disappointing to see the actual ships wheel looked more like the steering wheel from a cheap 1970's saloon car. The basic controls were replicated on flying bridges on either side of the ship. The ships wheels here were no more than the circumference of a baked bean can. The officer in charge of the delicate manoeuvre kept shouting commands to the helmsman.

"Why does he keep shouting "Pork pie with chips" asked my son Tom.

The officer patiently explained "I think you'll find that's "Port five" which basically means left a bit and the "with chips" bit is mid-ships which is nautical jargon for straight ahead. I was secretly glad it was Tom who had asked and not me.

They went on to show us a radar system that not only showed the position of every ship in the channel including us, but also where it would be in twelve minutes time assuming it maintained the same course and speed, therefore you could see a collision twelve minutes before it actually happened.

There was a system that automatically controlled speed. This basically made sure that we would arrive in Rotterdam exactly on time. There were systems that detected fire, systems that made it impossible to leave the berth without and all the sea doors being shut. Somebody lit a cigarette in their cabin whilst we were there. Security were dispatched to deal with the offender within seconds. They could even tell it was cigarette smoke from the instruments on the bridge as opposed to an actual fire.

All very reassuring and I wondered to myself if our vessel the previous year had the same sophisticated kit. I suspected not and decided not to share that thought. How did they keep the ship in line and not bump into the lock wall? Well, on the flying bridges there were portholes that looked downwards and on the glass someone had drawn a neat line with a chinagraph pencil. All we do is keep that line in line with the edge of the lock they explained. Amidst all the technical wizardry there is still space for a bit of basic geometry. We would have stayed there all night I suspect, except that we did need to eat.

We have done a lot of North Sea crossings from most ports on the east coast at one time or another. Folkestone, Dover, Felixstowe, Harwich, Hull, Newcastle have all been setting off points for us to either Zeebrugge, Rotterdam, Europoort, Hoek van Holland or Ijmuiden. These have all been to visit the Netherlands.

To understand why we fell in love with the Netherlands and why we didn't join the hoards who simply trek across the Low Countries on their way to somewhere else we need to go back much further in time to when we had a seven year old girl and a three year old boy. It's actually quite difficult thinking of a holiday you will all get something out of at those ages. Sure, you can go and lie on a beach but Gill and I were not very good at that, so we alighted on the idea of going to the Netherlands and cycling.

Tom could go on a child seat and as for Phillipa, well she would just have to peddle herself. I can't remember how impressed she was at the time, probably not very, but some years later when she had to propel herself on two wheels up a steep climb on a Duke of Edinburgh's award school trip somewhere she did have cause to thank me when she was the only one to make it to the top.

The first holiday we stayed near what was then a very small town of Harskamp. The site was huge but it didn't feel so. The reason for this was that all the pitches were set in glades or clearings in the forest. The larger ones might accommodate ten caravans, the smaller ones just two or three.

The site was very child friendly, other than to get your caravan on and off site cars were not allowed. You simply left your car on a large parking lot adjoining the site. Its raison d'etre was to showcase the wildlife of the surrounding forest and introduce children to the wonders of the natural world.

They did have a campfire meeting once a week, attended by two or three hundred campers at which they would sing songs mostly of course in Dutch. However, whilst we were there they touchingly included two or three songs in English especially for us, the only four English speakers on the site. I also had the humbling experience of sharing a beer with three Dutchman who spent the evening talking to me and to each other in English so as not to be exclusive. It made me realise how lazy we English are with languages.

In the town there was a petrol station where you could hire bikes incredibly cheaply for about £5 a week. The bikes were quite old but perfectly serviceable. There used to be shops like this all over the Netherlands. However they have over the years been replaced by far more upmarket establishments. Unfortunately although the bikes are state of the art, so are the prices and cheap bike hire is now a thing of the past.

Not many English go on camping or caravan holidays specifically to the Netherlands and so on that first trip we found that we were something of a novelty. For example, the roll-along style water carrier favoured by British caravaners is unheard of and certainly hitherto unseen on Dutch caravan sites. I found myself picking up quite a crowd of amused and impressed Dutchmen giving me thumbs up signs as I replenished our water supply. I began to understand how the guy who invented the wheel must have felt as he sailed past his fellow cavemen humping huge lumps of rock in their arms.

This was quite strange really because when you visit Dutch camping shops they are huge and stuffed with all manner of natty inventions that we never see this side of the channel. The Dutch are the largest caravan owning nation per capita in the world so you can see why I feel at home there. Suffice it to say we returned to the Netherlands for our holidays for many years, although we did visit many different parts of it.

One of our destinations was right over in the east of the Netherlands in the province of Drenthe. Not really a tourist hotspot, but a Dutchman once explained to me that a lot of older people go there for their holidays. I asked why and he replied "because it is so flat." without even a trace of irony.

The capital of the region is Groningen. A university town it deserves its reputation as one of the prettiest cities in the Netherlands. You are quite close to the German border, which is a couple of hours cycle ride away. You can also visit Westerbork, known as the Gateway to Hell. It was the transit camp where many Jewish prisoners spent their last night on Dutch soil before being transported further east to Auschwitz. Anne Frank was held here for a time. The camp which is now a museum was considered quite humane by Nazi standards. It contained shops and hairdressers for example. It was designed to give false hope to its occupants. It's quite chilling but well worth a visit.

If you have ever noticed the line of islands across the top of the Netherlands,these are the Wadden Islands. The smallest of which, Schiermonnikoog can be visited by ferry from Lauwersoog in the North of Drenthe. It's a pretty Island which doesn't allow motor vehicles so make sure you take your bike. I wouldn't recommend paddling in the sea though. Gill and Phillipa and Tom would undoubtedly counsel against this as well, since they were the ones that tried it. They went paddling through the muddy sand when all of a sudden the mud shifted alarmingly and out rose the smooth black writhing arch of a body of what was thought at the time to be the Loch Ness Monster also taking a break in the Netherlands, but what was probably just a very large eel. The screams could be heard in Loch Ness anyway.

Most of our days were spent cycling. If you don't

care much for cycling and you are in the Netherlands, then you truly are in hell. The Netherlands is the very last word in its provision for bicycles. In most situations and wherever possible bicycles and motor transport are separated. In Britain we have footpaths and bridleways. In the Netherlands they also have cycle paths or fietspads to use the Dutch word and if anything they are even more extensive than the footpath network.

Even in places we have visited several times we always find new tracks. You can be in the middle of nowhere, miles from the nearest town and there in forests, meadows and moorlands you will be cycling on a concrete or tarmacadam cycle path. At every junction there are direction and distance signs. It is incredible and must cost a fortune to maintain. It is however very well used.

The main reason for this is the Dutch attitude to cycling. Whilst they are in my experience some of the kindest, most helpful and tolerant people you will ever meet, all that goes out of the window when you get them on a bike. For then, there is a strict etiquette and no allowance is made for foreigners.

In the Netherlands the bicycle is king. Go to a supermarket and you will see more cycles in the bike racks than you will see cars in the car park, the same is true at the railway stations. As I said in most places bikes and other road users are segregated. Where cycle tracks intersect with roads it is the cars that must give way. Even when cars have the right of way they often cede this in favour of bikes.

If however a car driver has the temerity to occupy road space reserved for bikes there is no such reciprocation. I once observed a car which had stopped in the cycle track whilst waiting to turn left into a major road. An angry passing cyclist pressed his front tyre against the car door and stared the driver out whilst shouting dark curses at him which sounded like magic spells designed to turn the occupier of the car into a frog which could in turn be crushed under the front wheel of a passing bike.

There are two reasons for utter respect which cars show bikes. The first is that most Dutch motorists are also cyclists, therefore unlike their British counterparts they do not regard bikes as a nuisance that should be banished from the highway. The second is this, and here really is the thing, it is enshrined in their law. This declares that if as a motorist you are involved in an accident with a bicycle then it is your fault. No exceptions, no mitigating circumstances, it is your fault. On a bicycle you can happily clatter into the back of some one's spanking brand new Mercedes and make a right mess of it, or pull out in front of one, giving them no reasonable opportunity to stop, it will still be the car drivers fault. In the Netherlands, if you are involved in an accident with a bicycle, you are in big trouble.

Not all of the Dutch agree with this weighting of road traffic laws in favour of cyclists but it does mean of course that everyone is very careful around bikes. There are twenty three million bicycles in the Netherlands in a country with a population of seventeen million, so more bikes than people. For comparison, in this country there are a mere three million bikes. Although accidents are not unknown, when you consider the numbers of bicycles in the Netherlands it is rare to hear of lorries killing cyclists. That is because they are fitted with special mirrors that give the driver a clear view down the side of their wagon and they daren't not use them. That is what makes it such a fantastic place to take young children on a relaxing holiday. You only need to apply the tiniest modicum of common sense and everyone is perfectly safe.

Of course the topography helps. You tend not to get too many whinges about being tired or how far it is or even "are we nearly there yets" when it is such an easy landscape to cycle. Even arthritic old men like me can make it through a reasonable number of miles without feeling as if we are gasping our terminal breath.

The other great joy of cycling the Netherlands is that you can drink as much as you like of their excellent beer and never put a pound on. Seriously what's not to like and so after we discovered the Netherlands with only a few exceptions that was where we tended to take family holidays.

The Dutch don't especially like being referred to as Dutch. Don't get me wrong, no one is going to come and punch you in the nose for this faux pas or refuse to talk to you but they prefer to be referred to as Netherlanders or even Hollanders even though most of them aren't from Holland. I should clarify here that Holland refers to just two Northern provinces of the Netherlands, North Holland and confusingly South Holland.

Why they don't go in too much for Dutch I don't know, perhaps it sounds too much like Deutch or Duitse, which means German and many Dutch are not that fond of the Germans. They certainly don't like being mistaken for them. The word hasn't entirely been expunged from their language but when you see it, then it's usually as part of something written in English. For example, the KLM Jumbo jet which stands as an exhibit in the air museum at Lleystad is called "The Flying Dutchman"

One day whilst out walking I happened across a small van parked in a forest car park with advertisements for dog food on its rear. The signage on the side of the van read "Joanne's Doggy Services." As the Dutch word for dog is "hond" I found myself idly wondering just what sort of doggy services it was that Joanne actually provided. However, it's probably not quite so much fun as it sounds. In the Netherlands, strangely, most marketing catch-phrases are actually written in English, sometimes with unintended consequences.

This is a curious aspect of Dutch. You will be over-taken by a forty-foot wagon on the motorway, you will if you are towing a caravan with a Rover 400 anyway. The wagon complete with Dutch registration proudly display's the company's name, say "Van de Lader", , and underneath will be a tag line in English "The Netherlands favourite furniture movers" or something like that. Or you will see a quintessentially Dutch high street chain shop like Hema or Etos and written underneath will be a catchphrase such as "It's a beautiful day." Or you may see a factory with a corporate logo and the company's name followed by an English explanation what they do; Drieklomp - Suppliers of Veal to the rich and famous. Why? I have no idea, a good proportion of the audience won't understand it and apparently a good proportion of the Dutch resent their language being vandal-ised in this way.

My own personal favourite was a commercial radio station we used to pick up as we drove across the Netherlands. Now the radio in my car shows the name of the station which was unprom-isingly and unfortunately called FGM. The banner that streams underneath declares F****** Good Music. This word doesn't seem to have the same incendiary effect in the Netherlands. I've seen Christmas decorations for sale which proudly pronounce "F*** Christmas". However, I suppose that whatever the Dutch is for this particular Elizabethan curse it wouldn't have much effect if sprinkled liberally into written English either.

Whilst we are on the subject of marketing it should be noted that the names continental caravan manufacturers give to their caravans do not always translate well into English. Though amazingly some of them do market their products over here without giving a thought to tweaking the name. Thus it is not unknown to be overtaken by a vehicle towing a Deathleffs caravan. This is a German manufacturer and very fine vans I'm sure they are too but it does sound like an incurable disease one might pick up in a tropical swamp.

The Dutch have a manufacturer called Kip, now I suppose that might work in English, kip equals sleep equals caravan to sleep in, but in Dutch it means Chicken. I imagine some hapless salesman somewhere, with his head in hands trying to figure out how to sell a caravan with the unappealing name of Chicken Shack.

I have also seen caravans proudly bearing the legend Eriba Puck, presumably some slightly deviant sex position. There are also Lord Munsterlands, Wilps and the magnificently named Weltbummlers out there. I'm sure none of these can be easy to persuade potential customers to part with their hard earned cash for. I'm not making any of this up. I am sure it is only a matter of time before some enterprising continental caravan manufacturer comes up with the all new - Covid 19.

I sometimes have this recurring nightmare where I am at a reception being hosted by the Caravan Club. Waiters are carrying small glasses of dry sherry around on silver salvers among the invited members. A very smartly dressed member from the upper echelons of the club approaches me. He has a huge white handlebar moustache is and wearing a green Caravan Club blazer complete with emblem of the club emblazoned in silver and gold across his breast pocket. His white shirt and club tie are so blindingly immaculate you dare not look at them too long for fear of damaging your eyesight. He opens his mouth and in a very upper class growl says "I say old boy I just changed my van to a twin axle, fur lined, ocean going, twenty four carat, luxury, executive platinum edition you know. What is it you tow?"

I reply in a very small Stressed Eric sort of a voice "A Chicken Shack"

My sherry glass is removed from my hand and placed on a Formica tray. I walk slump shouldered towards the door. I am slow hand clapped all the way. At the door the chairman advises me that I am never to darken the portals of the Caravan Club's East Grinstead headquarters again, ever! At this point I usually wake up in a cold sweat, so fortunately I never find out what happens to me after this.

One of the great difficulties of trying to learn to speak Dutch, and as we shall see there are many, is that nearly everyone you meet will try to speak English to you. Most Dutch speak English very well, especially the younger ones who learn in school and even have lessons other than English taught in English. Can you imagine the uproar if the education secretary announced that henceforth all Physics lessons will be taught in Spanish or Chinese? Yet this is exactly what they do with their smarter students. Little wonder that their vocabulary is amazing.

The thing with Dutch is that you try a few halting words and whilst the natives are genuinely appreciative of the fact that you try, they can't understand you and you certainly can't understand their reply. I have a theory that this isn't entirely your fault. The thing that makes the language so difficult is the pronunciation. British mouths just don't seem to have all the parts necessary to speak the words correctly. The Dutch even seem to understand this themselves.

I once tried to book a table at a restaurant. Not unreasonably the maître de asked me to spell my name. After weeks of practice I had actually learned to do this in Dutch. When I came to the last letter, which is a "Y" I proudly enunciated something which sounds a bit like "eegrek" but the "gr" sound is made in the back of the throat. He raised his hand to his heart, looked me in the eye and said "Respect" and he meant it. It was big moment for me.

The next great difficulty is that the Dutch are unbelievably pedantic about pronunciation, at least from our point of view. I once visited one of the national parks, De Hoge Veleuwe which is pronounced something like "De Hokay Felouver". On our return some Dutch friends asked us where we had been that day. I had anticipated this, and having listened and practiced all day "De Hokay Felouver" I faithfully intoned. Our Dutch friends looked at me and then at each other with puzzled expressions. I repeated what I had just said several more times, changing the emphasis slightly, raising and lowering the tone, and being English, probably the volume.

Each time they looked at me more and more puzzled. Eventually, in desperation, I got my map out and pointed to the place. "Ahh they cried in unison, at what was once unclear came into perfect focus "De Hokay Felouver" they said.
"That was what I said wasn't it?" I practically shouted, my frustration evident.

The Dutch language feels impossible to learn yet I do not understand why this should be. A lot of their words are identical to the English. Even those that aren't have a kind of eccentric English onomatopoeic logic to them. For example the Dutch for Frogs is "Kikkers" and a spider is a "spiner." As you drive into a dark, forest shaded, stretch of road you will see signs exhorting you to "onsteek uw Lichten". The Dutch equivalent of, no trespassing is "Verboden Toegang" but you can't help thinking "Forbidden gangway for toes" can you? Electric fences carry the dire warning "Skriek Draad" usually accompanied by a skull and crossbones. I've no idea what it means but "Dreadful Shriek" can't be that wide of the mark. In any event it doesn't sound good. It doesn't always work. The "slagerij" is the local butchers shop and "slagroom" is whipped cream. No onomatopoeic logic there, unless you have particularly unusual tastes anyway.

Famously John F Kennedy when visiting the Netherlands had a conversation with the then Dutch foreign minister Joseph Luns. The story goes that when JFK asked Luns about his hobbies, he answered: "I fok horses." The Dutch verb "fokken" means "to breed," which is basically what he was trying to say. When Kennedy replied, "Pardon?" Luns responded enthusiastically, "Yes, paarden!" ("Paarden" means "horses" in Dutch.). Incidentally, knowing what you now know, you're not entirely surprised to learn that "fokken" means to breed are you?

There are other words and phrases in Dutch sound like English but mean something entirely different. "You can...." translates as "U kunt...." and it is unfortunately pronounced exactly as you would think. Unlike the island off Hong Kong, you can't silence a second letter, to avoid upsetting your maiden aunt, there are no alternatives it's, "U Kunt". Now get used to it.

When you visit a tourist attraction the usually very pleasant and welcoming staff in the reception area of whatever it is you happen to be visiting will often describe all the things you can do whilst you are there. Unfortunately, due I think in part the syntax of Dutch grammar this takes the form of a list with a new sentence for each item. For the sake of your maiden aunt I'll give the example in English:
"You can visit the museum"
"You can visit the sculpture park"
"You can go to the coffee shop"
"You can use the white bicycles"
"You can join the nature tour"
I could go on but I think you get the picture.

If I've given the impression that Dutch is merely an eccentric form of English in which the words all look the same but are just pronounced differently then, this would not be entirely true. In an effort to improve my Dutch language skills I read some Dutch books as this is one of the best ways to learn how the language is actually used. These are mainly children's books where the language is fairly simple. My current reading is called "De Gekke Loempia" which translates as "The Mad Indonesian Spring Roll."

Putting it all together it is amazing that the Brits and the Dutch get along as well as we seem to. Personally I'm surprised that there hasn't been a major diplomatic incident. Though I do sometimes idly wonder if this is why Brexit negotiations went so badly.

Apart from the language some cultural differences become most obvious when you go to the supermarket. I have on occasion when shopping needed to buy toilet rolls. It fascinates me that what I would have thought would be a homogenous product the world over can be so vastly different in different countries. In the Netherlands the tool with which to perform the essential paperwork is both narrower and about half the size of a standard loo roll here in the UK. It also comes with a series of instructions for its correct use complete with diagrams on the wrapper. Now I suppose that at some time in my life, though I can't remember it, I must have been taught to use toilet tissue. I assume this is the same for everyone, which begs the question; who on earth reads these? An even more prescient question is; who on earth writes them and why? I have visions of stormy project meetings at Unilever where they argue and thrash out precise wordings. Perhaps they have focus groups of end users, (so to speak!) where they show them alternative proposed diagrams to approve in order to convey the vital messages most accurately. Perhaps the final version needs board approval? We shall never know, but perhaps the most interesting question of all is why someone deems it necessary to give the Dutch such helpful guidance, when the English speaking nations are denied the same assistance.

One place where my halting grasp of the language has frequently caused problems is eating out. To be fair Dutch Cuisine isn't always to our taste.

129

There are some very nice upmarket restaurants but at the other end of the scale virtually everything is fried. I once ordered what I thought were ham and egg sandwiches for us all. What arrived was four lots of fried ham each with three eggs on the top.

Ever supportive my wife and offspring refused to eat any of it, but we didn't want to cause offence so I was required to eat as much as possible. Whilst they tucked into the cakes we had also ordered I worked my way through twelve eggs. Still, in a caravan, I got my revenge later that night, but - now how can I put this delicately, – I had no use for toilet paper for some considerable time.

There are a lot of Indonesian restaurants in the Netherlands, a leftover from the days when the Dutch had a significant empire in the Far East. In attempting to translate from Indonesian to Dutch to English I have managed to order some truly disgusting things to eat.

Chief amongst them was something called Kip Satyr which I was reliably informed was skewered chicken in a nut sauce. It may well have been, but it looked like dog turds liberally coated with viscous diarrhea. I looked at Gill hopefully, wondering if she might want to do a swap for her tasty looking curry. Gill, who is even more finicky than me about what she puts in her mouth, snapped "Absolutely not!" before I'd even got the question out of my mouth. I don't know what a dog turd coated with viscous diarrhea tastes like, or maybe I do because after two mouthfuls, I got up went to the loo and deposited the entire contents of my stomach, only a very small part of which was kip satyr.

After this incident we only ever dared to order something called Kai Tin, a spicy chicken dish served with rice. It got so bad, that at one restaurant they ceased to bring us a menu and just automatically served us Kai Tin, every time we rocked up.

We didn't always take our caravan to the Netherlands, especially when I was still working. There were a few reasons why this might be the case. Sometimes we would go at the Autumn half-term when we could rent a holiday home for a lower or similar price than it would cost to take the van and all without the attendant risks of towing in what might be less than clement weather conditions.

It was on one such trip that on our way home we realised that we were going to arrive ridiculously early at Rotterdam - Europoort for the overnight ferry home. Thus we got off the motorway at a place called Nunspeet, I bought a cycling map from the VVV (Tourist Information Centre) and hastily planned a couple of hours ride round this very beautiful part of the Netherlands.

I should add at this point that by this stage our by now teenage children were only coming with us for part of a holiday. Trying to gently let us down I think for the not too distant time when they would not come at all. The property where we had spent our holiday in the small town of Hieno boasted that bicycles were included and indeed they were. However, Tom, having seen previous examples of the types of bike the Dutch provided for free had insisted on bringing his own. Gill for not dissimilar reasons had made the same demand. This meant that we were in the fortunate position of having two bikes, precariously hanging from a boot mounted cycle carrier. All we needed to kill a couple of hours and break our journey home.

Now Gill's was her own bike so that was fine. Tom who would have been around thirteen at the time had I suppose a three quarter size mountain bike which was probably getting a bit small for him. By this time he didn't use it that much, except on holiday and it was certainly too small for me. I couldn't really be bothered to adjust it for what after all was merely going to be a couple of hours cycling punctuated by lunch. So we must have looked a bit odd as we hit the track with Gill on a sensible lady's bike and me swearing as I hit my knees on the handlebars and wobbled away on what must have looked like a stolen bike in hot pursuit of my more elegantly mounted wife. Somehow we made it round my carefully planned, circular cycle route. On the way we found the ideal place for a holiday the following year. It was even worth the bruised kneecaps.

The ideal place happened to be some one's private garden and amazingly they took our booking. Thus began a friendship which exists to this day with Jan and Tineke. Actually their "garden" was a former paddock which had been landscaped and also contained three small holiday homes. There was also space for three caravans complete with water supply, mains electricity shower and toilet facilities. It was really like a very private Certificated Location. In those days they used the caravan pitches for family and so we hired one of the holiday homes, but as the years passed and they found permanent tenants for the holiday homes we took our caravan and pitched in their garden.

By the time we visited the following year Phillipa had stopped coming with us in favour of holidaying with friends. It was in preparation for this that I decided to have a fatherly chat with her about the dangers of drugs, which went something like this.

"Pippa, do you ever come across drugs at school?"

"Yeah of course" she tutted in that tone which sixteen year old girls use to inform you that they have just been asked the stupidest question in the world, which she probably had been.

"Well what sort of drugs do you come across?" I enquired.

"Mostly weed" she replied in bored tone of voice that suggested she knew where this conversation was going.

"Weed?" I questioned. I must confess to being pretty naive when it comes to narcotics.

Another tut. "Cannabis dad"

"Well what do you do with the cannabis?" I enquired.

"Well most people mix it with tobacco and smoke it but some of them make slow boats, but they're usually sick when they do that."

"…and what's a slow boat?"

Phillipa explained how you made one from an empty cola tin and compass, the sort normally used for drawing circles. I'll spare you the detail lest there be some law about explaining such things in print, but I was a little shocked to find that my little girl knew all about this.

Hoping it would be beyond her financial resources I asked "How much does weed cost?"

"Five quid for half an eighth."

"Half an eighth?" I quizzed by now wishing I'd never started this conversation.

Another tut. "Half an eighth of an ounce dad! Look

I can get you some if you want some?" she said in a voice betraying her exasperation with the discussion.

Interesting as it was to note that in the metric age "weed" is supplied in imperial quantities, I decided not to question her any further. She assured me that she didn't do drugs and I chose to believe her.

She is now a school teacher herself and has two children of her own. Perhaps she will be better equipped to have these kind of discussions with them or of course the world may have moved on.

Tom still came on holiday with us that year and brought one of his friends with him. We thought they would go off and do their own thing but they pretty much stuck with us for the whole holiday.

However the following year was the year of the credit crunch, along with a lot of people I was worried about my job and so we didn't go to the Netherlands that year or the year after. By the time we felt secure enough to renew our acquaintance, Phillipa and Tom had other plans. They have both however since spent holidays out there with their own families.

IN PRAISE
OF UNLOVED
BRITAIN

If a man is tired of Milton Keynes then he is tired
of life as Samuel Johnson didn't quite say, but I'm
sure he would have done had it been built back
then. I make no apology for the fact that what follows is a Hymn to Milton Keynes, a sort of love
poem.

Most people when I tell them of my affection for
the elegant Buckinghamshire City, with its wide
tree lined boulevards and get all misty eyed, look
at me with the same disbelief with which they regard me with when I tell them I love caravanning.

It's soulless they tell me, all concrete and roundabouts. When I ask them if they have ever actually
been, they usually reply in the negative, but as-

sure me that they have heard all about it. Well not from me they haven't. Milton Keynes is a fantastic place for all the reasons I am about to elucidate. For those of you doubting my endowing Milton Keynes with the accolade of city, I should point out that the royal seal of approval for this status was given on 22nd February 2018.

For several years I worked in Milton Keynes doing a weekly commute there from the Wirral, a distance of 168 miles precisely. Believe me, I do know this, every last cone on the M6 of it.

When one day I suggested to Gill that we take the caravan and have a holiday there, she looked at me suspiciously. After wondering if I had a mistress there, she reluctantly agreed to go. We had a great time and I am pleased to report that she too is now also a firm fan of the place.

So what is it that makes this much derided corner of England such a great place to go? Let's start from the centre and work our way out. There are no high rise buildings in the centre of MK which makes it very light and open city. At one time nothing was allowed to be built which was higher than the cathedral dome, regrettably I think they have transgressed this rule in more recent years, but it still feels a light, safe place to be. No one is going to film dark crime dramas here anytime soon.

Over the last fifty years the six rows of trees that line the sides and centres of the main boulevards have grown up making it what must be the greenest looking city centre you will ever see, an effect added to by the many parks and garden squares littered across the city.

The centre of Milton Keynes is organised into three main areas; the business district, the shopping district, and the theatre district. On a summer evening the theatre district with its bars and restaurants outside dining and drinking areas has a great convivial atmosphere. You can sit watching people hurrying to the theatre or the cinema, enjoy a drink or something to eat, watch the stars come out, the lights twinkle through the canopy of trees and just enjoy the buzz.

Beyond the theatre district is Campbell Park, partly formal and partly a country park. There is a climb up to a view point where at one side you can see the silver ribbon of the Grand Union canal threading its way through the country side.

The opposite view is back towards the city centre is down Midsummer Boulevard. In a small nod to the mystical and a riposte to detractors who say MK has no soul, two of the three main boulevards in the centre are named Avebury Boulevard and Silbury Boulevard respectively after the druid worship sites in Wiltshire. Midsummer Boulevard is not; however, it was built so that on Mid-summers day the sun rises exactly in line with it. Milton Keynes may the sun never set on you.

The shopping district has a large array of shops most of which are contained within two under-cover centres. There is a bustling outdoor market which is open every day selling anything from fresh bread to antique cutlery.

The business district is lower down the hill close to the railway station. It is I suppose the first thing people see when they get off a train and I wonder if in part this is what gives Milton Keynes its un-deserved reputation. The business district is like a business park anywhere, it is composed of office buildings which are never going to be that inter-esting to anyone other than the people who work in them. Unfortunately for many business vis-itors that is all they will ever see.

According to Billy Liar a man can lose himself in London. Well he certainly can't in Milton Keynes. The road system is built on a grid. All the roads running north to south are numbered V1 to V11 from left to right and all of the roads running east to west are numbered H1 to H10 starting at the top. At every intersection there is a round-about. Therefore, so long as you have even a basic understanding of geometry, you know the difference between horizontal and veritical, and you can count, then getting from any one place to any other place is easy.

I make this point because of the number of people who tell me it's impossible to drive through MK without getting lost. No it isn't. Now go back to school and learn some basic maths. I will concede there are a lot of roundabouts, a 124 of them to be precise, which is the most of any town or city in the UK, but only very rarely do you encounter a traffic jam in Milton Keynes so even this is a good thing.

The other huge plus point is that all of the roads have separate cycle tracks at the side of them. At the roundabouts they disappear down under-passes and emerge at the other side. This is like cycling in the Netherlands without being in the Netherlands.

The cycle tracks don't stop at the main roads either. There are tracks that run through the housing areas and the parks, there is a track, converted from an old railway that takes you all the way to Newport Pagnell, the entire Grand Union canal towpath has been made into a good quality cycle track. Welcome to Britain's only city that was truly built for cycling.

Finally, let's visit the housing areas where people actually live and someone really did think about this as a place for people to live. The houses are not obvious, they are mostly screened from the arterial roads by thick lines of trees, twenty-two million of them, that's more than a hundred per resident. If you look for it, you can even find a cathedral of trees not far from Willen Lake and it really is worth going to see.

The trees kill the sound from the main roads and again make this a very green peaceful place to live. No one living in Milton Keynes is ever more than half a mile from green space. Every district has a local centre which always has a church, a pub, a park with children's play area and a selection of shops.

There is also a fair old selection of public art, famously the concrete cows of course but much else too. The old villages that were swallowed up by Milton Keynes have been tastefully preserved and incorporated into the infrastructure including the original village of Milton Keynes itself. Scattered through this residential paradise are fifteen lakes and eleven miles of canals giving Milton Keynes more bridges than Venice and more shoreline than the entire coast of Jersey.

We have visited Milton Keynes several times and stayed at a Certificated Location close to Stony Stratford and thus my caravanning career came full circle. You will recall that's CLs are sites for just five caravans. This one was run by quite an eccentric lady who could never remember whether you had paid her or not. We always did, on the basis that we wanted to come back and you never knew if she might suddenly remember and present me with a large bill.

On one occasion we invited Gill's sisters and husbands to come and stay at the bed and breakfast which she also ran. Unfortunately, she could never remember whether she had given them breakfast or not. In the end she just left some cereals, bread and jams out and told them to get their own breakfast.

One of the great things is that you can cycle pretty much anywhere round here, so seldom do you need to get the car out. By this time our children had long flown the nest, but we still had a dog to keep us company on our travels who would run along at the side of the bike, provided you didn't go too fast.

One place really worth a visit is Bletchley Park, home to the World War II code breakers and the National Computer Museum. Famously of course this is where the Enigma and Lorenz codes were broken thus shortening the war by an estimated two years. You see, as if Milton Keynes didn't have enough going for it, it also won the war and without it there might never have been an electronic programmable computer. So there!

The National Computing Museum is a must if you grew up as computers were just entering everyday life. In here you will find some of the first popular pocket calculators, Sinclair Spectrums, BBC Acorns and a host of other stuff that reminds you that we didn't always carry computers around in our pockets. You will also find a rebuilt Colossus, the world's first semi-programmable computer, without which the Lorenz code would never have been cracked.

It was invented by a man called Tommy Flowers a Post Office engineer. It always seems incredible to me that a man who in effect shortened the war by around two years, saving millions of lives and in many ways bequeathed the world the computer age is someone of whom most people have never heard. There are no statues of him or buildings named after him and despite his genius he never became a wealthy man or received much credit during his lifetime. This is in no small measure due to the extreme secrecy that surrounded the work of Bletchley Park, but it still seems desperately unfair.

The same is true of Bill Tutte, a brilliant mathematician, whose breakthrough in working out how the Lorenz code could be broken thus enabling Flowers machine to do the number crunching is virtually unknown today. Neither Flowers or Tutte ever received any honour or award from their own country. After the war Tutte emigrated to Canada. The more enlightened Canadians did give Tutte the Order of Canada medal for out-standing talent and exceptional contribution to humanity.

Even the considerably more famous Alan Tur-ing received little recognition for his remarkable achievements during his short lifetime. Without his invention of the Bombe machine, of which you can see a replica at Bletchley Park the Enigma code would probably have remained impene-trable. Turing sadly took his own life biting an apple laced with cyanide following a brush with the law over his homosexuality. When I find out about these things it makes me very sad because I wonder how much more quickly the computer age would have come had such men been recog-nised for their achievements and allowed to de-velop their ideas.

Milton Keynes is also home to The Open Uni-versity, the world's first degree-awarding distance learning institution. Less eruditely but probably more importantly for most people it is also home to the UKs first ever multiplex cinema. It is also the place where the saviour of winter motorists comes from, WD40. The WD stands for "Water Dis-placement" and allegedly only six people in the world know the precise formula, which unsurprisingly was perfected at the fortieth attempt.

There you go two thousand positive words about Milton Keynes, if this hasn't been done before then it jolly well ought to have been. I tell you if Milton Keynes Development Corporation ever find out about me I will be on the front cover of their magazine.

****

Whilst we are on the subject of unloved Britain, I'd like to pay a brief tribute to Hull, yes you did read that correctly, Hull. For many years all I saw of Hull was the road in. Clive Sullivan Way, which is what the M62, at its eastern most end, magically turns into without you noticing.

Clive Sullivan was a rugby player who played for both Hull Kingston Rovers and Hull Rugby Football Club who sadly died aged only forty-two from cancer.

I also saw a bridge over a large patch of mud, the River Hull apparently, and the entrance to Hull Prison, high security apparently. Shortly after the prison I'd turn right into the St Georges Dock to board the overnight ferry to Rotterdam so my knowledge of Hull was even sketchier than my knowledge of music.

All that was to change however when one-day Gill won a night away in an Hotel, courtesy of Bernard Matthews Turkey Roast. The prize was a weekend away in any Holiday Inn in the UK and we chose Hull. Yes, the girl on the phone at Bernard Matthews sounded pretty incredulous too.

"I know this is a turkey company" she said "but that doesn't mean we want you to have a holiday that's one"

"Hull" she repeated "H-U-L-L as in Kingston upon, East Yorkshire."

"Yes, the one on the marina." I confirmed.

"Well I'll tell you what then. We will give you a second room free for the children." She said in a voice dripping with sympathy. I can only assume that hotel rooms were not that much in demand in Hull that particular weekend. I put the phone down, reflecting that there was now someone else who thought I was slightly mad and she didn't even know that I had a caravan.

On the way into Hull we stopped just off Clive Sullivan's ubiquitous Way because I wanted to walk over the Humber Bridge. "Why?" asked the children in that whiney tone of voice that also tells you they really don't want to walk over the Humber Bridge.

I tried to sell it, I really did. I explained that as a youth I used to go sailing in Grimsby and I watched it being built. That the road way sections were bought in with the road markings already painted on them and they put it together like a gigantic Lego set. I told them how it was once the world's largest single span suspension bridge. How the towers were so far apart that they pointed slightly away from each other to match the curvature of the Earth.

They were singularly unimpressed as was Gill. I had been hoping for a better response from my spouse, especially as her father had been a Cambridge graduate of engineering and Chief Engineer at British Steel Corporation. Unfortunately, he had neglected to pass that particular gene on to his daughter.

To be fair the good people of Hull were not that impressed with their new bridge either at the time which they regarded as something of a white elephant. My editor, who lived in the area for some years tells me it was known locally as the "Bridge to Nowhere" as the planned connecting motorways did not get built until many years later. Today however it is a grade I listed building.

Reluctantly, the three of them traipsed after me across the Humber Bridge as I regaled them with yet more fascinating facts about this remarkable structure. When we got to approximately the half way point, the requests to go back became even more strident, but I put my foot down. "I haven't come all this way to walk *halfway* over the Humber Bridge" I bellowed, slightly more loudly than I intended. After that the journey continued in silence and I comforted myself by thinking about all the things my offspring would now never know about the Humber Bridge.

Following the somewhat unpromising start things looked up. You wouldn't believe all the things there are to see and do on a wet winter weekend in Hull, and most of them are for free. After the debacle of the bridge I thought I had better make amends so we went to a fish and chip café on the Hessle Road and had what remain for me the best fish and chips I have ever eaten, all washed down with mugs of Yorkshire tea.

We went on to the Street Life Museum which is a kind of transport museum, but you are allowed to clamber on the buses, trucks and horse coaches. They have mannequins sat on them with speakers attached so they appear to tell you about their lives. There is even a sort of fairground ride in which you are tossed up and down in the darkness while clinging to a mock candle. This is to give you some idea of what it was like riding the York to Hull mail coach back in the day, when potholes in road were nearly as bad as they are now.

They have constructed a whole street within which many of the exhibits are accommodated. It is a fantastic place, the children even forgot about the Humber Bridge experience, although they have reminded me of it many times since. Behind the Street Life Museum is the Arctic Corsair, a fishing trawler which has been converted into a floating museum about the fishing industry. Along the road is the William Wilberforce Museum and the Maritime Museum. Wilberforce was Hull's Member of Parliament for four years from 1780. There is also the fish trail to follow all around historic Hull which the children loved.

Hull Marina is these days full of expensive sailing

craft and state of the art motor launches. It is also home to the Holiday Inn where we were accommodated and fed that weekend. It has a good leisure and fitness centre complete with swimming pool which my lot found infinitely more diverting than the Humber Bridge, thus we spent our entire Sunday morning in there before heading back home.

Since our weekend in Hull which would have been circa 1995 the very impressive aquarium, The Deep has been built. We have been, it is indeed quite something, and at least when we were there very under visited. In 1999 Hull Corporation was briefly the richest local authority in the UK, following the flotation of what had been its own telephone company on the stock exchange. For some reason Hull was never served by BT. It spent part of the proceeds on building the deep. The windfall was £257 million, so it's not surprising that it's an impressive place.

Before we leave Hull I feel duty bound to declare an interest in promoting it so unreservedly. Hull and environs are home to more caravan manufacturers than anywhere else in the UK. This includes the UKs largest producer Swift Group. It also includes ABI, Delta, Europa, Willerby and proving the Europeans don't have the complete market in unpromisingly named caravans, Corona Caravans.

Wonderful though Milton Keynes and Hull are, and I am hoping I have left you in no doubt on this particular point, there are of course lots of other equally wonderful places, well maybe not quite equally, but still very fine places to visit in the UK with or without a caravan. So next up on our agenda we will go to Malmesbury, Wiltshire, spiritual home of the Dyson vacuum cleaner, though they are not actually made there anymore. It is also famous for the World of Music Arts and Dance festival of which we will hear more later, but let's get there first.

A car breakdown is never a pleasant experience and as most drivers will know it can be a dangerous one. Breaking down with caravan attached is not great either. I suppose in theory you can drop the legs and make a cup of tea whilst you wait for the recovery services to arrive but in practice you rarely come to a sickening halt in a place where this is possible.

Fortunately, this has only happened to me once in my adult life, although a certain Ford Cortina

153

imprinted indelible scars on my impressionable childhood mind. We had just left the M5 and were heading up Birdlip Hill in Gloucestershire. Half way up and without warning, the car lost all power and we just stopped. They were completing some roadworks at the time and what would normally have been the crawler lane was sealed off, thus we succeeded in closing the road for a brief period, until Gloucestershire's finest turned up and opened the inside lane to allow traffic to pass. I'm not sure if we made the local travel news that early afternoon but it wouldn't surprise me if we did.

It's not the only time I have been subject to abuse for having the temerity to tow a caravan down the English highway but the vitriol with which the invective was discharged that day was in a league of its own. I know it's frustrating to be caught in a traffic queue, but clearly a significant number of people must have considered that I had stopped there to admire the view from half-way up Birdlip Hill and beauteous though the Gloucestershire countryside is from this particular vantage point, I honestly hadn't.

Two of the guys working on the roadworks used

one of their vehicles to tow us to a safer spot whilst we waited for the recovery services. One of them was a good looking young man in his twenties with whom I think Gill secretly fell in love. She kept going on about what nice eyes he had for days anyway.

Eventually a recovery vehicle arrived, manned by a Polish chap, with less compelling eyes, whom I'm not entirely convinced was sober. I cannot be certain of this as he didn't have a lot of English and I don't know what slurring sounds like in Polish. At all events he towed us at breakneck and terrifying speed to our destination taking a good few wrong turnings along the way as he had difficulty interpreting both his satnav and our strangulated screams.

Improbably, we arrived safely, the only damage being a broken wing mirror on his recovery vehicle which had slammed into a house wall that someone had inconsiderately left too close to the road. I may not know what slurring sounds like in Polish but I think I've got the hang of swearing. Seriously, at the time, we were pleased he'd actually noticed the crunch at all.

When we had stopped shaking we set up the caravan and two very large Gin and Tonics and in this case they do deserve the capitalisation. We decided that the only way our recovery driver could cope with his own driving was to be permanently pissed and we needed to see if it would work for us. It did, Gill won over £300 on the National Lottery that evening.

The following morning, whilst we were still nursing sore heads the RAC arrived to see if they could repair the car on site. They couldn't. The car was taken away to a dealership in Stroud and that was the last time I saw it for three months. The leasing company thankfully provided us with a Ford Fiesta so we could enjoy the remainder of the holiday. It wasn't going to pull the caravan home, but that was two weeks away so we didn't need to worry about it or so we thought. At that time, we didn't know that the car would also be taking an extended break.

We stayed on a Certificated Location at a dairy farm near Malmesbury. I can honestly say I have learned a huge amount about the various types of farming in this country from staying at CLs on farms. Did you know for instance that cows are only dangerous when either they have young to protect or are in need of serving? Now I'll let you work out the meaning of serving for yourself, but if you've ever come across a herd of frisky cows in a field, it really does feel as if they are trying to find out if you are up to the job. Of course this also brings an entirely new meaning to the phrase, "Are you being served."

Our CL had some pretty unusual guests. If you have ever wondered what happened to the twenty-something pot smoking, peace loving, laid-back hippies of the sixties, well I am pleased to report that some of them at least became the eighty-something, pot smoking, peace loving, laid back hippies of the noughties. I know this because they turned up in their psychedelic campervans painted in designs that could only have been dreamed of after taking some mind expanding substances. Put it this way I doubt they appeared as options in the original brochure.

They were attending the World of Music Dramatic Art and Drama (WOMAD) festival which was taking place nearby. We know, we heard it and pretty "far out" it sounded too. Whilst no one actually got up and danced naked round their campfire, I have to say it is pretty disconcerting to see people vaguely reminiscent of your grandmother moving around in floaty diaphanous dresses muttering seductively at the moon in what I'm guessing were attempts at eroticism. However, each to their own and if you passed them in the late evening they were agreeable enough. "Peace man" or something like it, they would utter in a voice reminiscent of Dillon the rabbit from the Magic Roundabout. If you passed them in the morning, then they would utter nothing, they weren't there – for any of it!

Wiltshire is pretty, exceptionally so. It is also very varied from gently rolling hills to the upper reaches of the Thames to the dark Savernake Forest. One day, while Gill went shopping, I went in search of the source of the Thames and found it or at least I think I did. The one I found was in a field, near the village of Kemble and there is a big stone there that tells you this, so I'm not on my own. However, unbelievably, for one of our greatest rivers, the source is disputed. Some believe the source to be eleven miles further north at seven springs, which would make it the longest river in the UK. More fair minded authorities however would advise that seven springs is the source of the River Churn which joins the Thames at Cricklade in Wiltshire.

It has to be said that apart from the stone the field near Kemble is a pretty unimpressive site. It is a field with a slight depression in it. I am told that in winter the depression is sometimes gets a bit soggy. When I was there it was bone dry although there was a plank laid carelessly over the depression which I suppose is technically the first bridge over the Thames.

You may be wondering how we got home, given that our car was stuck in Stroud pending the arrival of some part or other from Eastern Europe. Well the answer is my good old dad rescued us. He was by this time in his late seventies but nevertheless, he and my mum drove all the way from Sheffield and the four of us then returned to The Wirral together.

Fortunately, he was still caravanning and therefore had a car with a tow bar. I did eventually have my car returned to me in full mechanical working order. It was also returned with a spanking brand new and very specifically V-shaped prang in the tailgate. When I pointed out to the delivery driver that this had not been there when I left it with them, he looked at it and said "Oh yes, that will have been done on the back wall of our compound." Garages hey? God love 'em, which is probably a good job because no one else does.

On another year when we chose not to go to The Netherlands we spent our summer holiday in Oxfordshire. Considerably further West at Henley the River Thames is a rather more impressive affair. Henley is a pleasant town best known for its famous regatta and the fact that it is a very popular spot for some of our better known celebrities to live. This is probably to do with its proximity to London.

During our whole time there we never saw anyone we recognised but there are indeed some impressively splendid houses in and around Henley that look as if they should belong to celebrities. There are any number of very pretty villages in this part of England The village of Turville, where the Vicar of Dibley was filmed is around here. There are one or two graves of the rich and famous in the cemetery.

We stayed on a CL in the village of Ibstone which afforded beautiful views over the Chilterns. In the evening Red Kites would swoop over us in huge numbers. The five caravans were arranged so that everyone had an unimpeded view. That was until one couple decided they wanted to do their own thing and plonk their caravan randomly in the middle of this perfect vista. To be fair I think they were having difficulty in pitching and I don't know what was going on in their lives at the time. They had a fearsome, brutal and very public row in which missiles were thrown and this resulted in them just leaving their van at an eccentric angle in the middle of the field. It was left to the site owner to come and sort it out. Brave man. The couple left the following morning having provided an entire evening's entertainment for the rest of us.

One favourite CL we used to visit quite a lot was at a vicarage just outside Congleton in Cheshire. Now Cheshire is stuffed with some very pretty towns and villages and I guess Congleton would not come top of most people's lists were they to compile one, but we liked it. Not all of Cheshire is flat by any means but large parts of it are and therefore eminently suitable for lazy cyclists. What this does mean is that you can go a fair old way along the country lanes on a bike without being completely exhausted. Alderley Edge,

Holmes Chapel, Chelford and the famous radio telescope at Jodrell Bank are all within reach, although some of them are easier reaches than others.

Our CL was run by the local vicar who has since retired. Vicarages can actually be quite dangerous places since they are prone to being visited by some unusual and quite disturbed characters at all sorts of odd hours of the night. They therefore often have some extra security devices around them. One evening after dark I went to the loo which was in one of the outbuildings. As I approached I triggered a bright security light. I saw the vicar through the lounge window get up and rush out of the house. Not wanting to be identified as the culprit who had disturbed him from writing his sermon, I turned and ran the other way round the main house setting off another security light. The vicar came in hot pursuit. I dodged into the loo and remained there silently until the coast was clear.

Gill had a commanding view from the caravan window of me playing hide and seek with the vicar. When I emerged some minutes later I glanced over to the caravan where in the lit window she was giving me signals as to which way to go round. The vicar by this time had gone back in doors.

Pressing myself close to the wall I followed her direction. Just when I had nearly made it back to the caravan field an enormous arc light shone on me. For those of you more musically aware than I, it was like the album cover of Paul McCartney and Wings, Band On The Run.

The Vicar once again came running out of the house. I dodged quickly into the bushes, whilst he vainly searched for me. By this time, I really did not want to meet him. I peered towards the caravan in the hope of further guidance from Gill over how best to escape.

She however was doubled up with laughter and absolutely no use at all. I remained hidden and prayed until I heard the vicar return to his house, presumably having uttered a fair few prayers himself. I eventually made it back to the caravan after a long muddy crawl through the undergrowth. I arrived back looking slightly dishevelled. If I had hoped for a hero's welcome from my wife I would have been disappointed, she couldn't stop laughing for the remainder of the evening. Even after we had gone to bed she occasionally woke up chuckling to herself. I felt bad for not fessing up and probably scaring the vicar and his wife half to death, but I never did. If per chance he ever reads this, I'd like to say I'm sorry, very, very sorry! It won't happen again.

In our early caravanning career, we used to spend a lot of time in the hills around Church Stretton in South Shropshire. It's not called little Switzerland for nothing. The glaciated valleys are sufficiently steep sided to be spectacular but not so high that you cannot get young children to climb them.

We found a small quiet commercial site here owned by an Austrian couple. He had been a mathematical engineer of some description and this quality came out in pretty much everything he did. He built the toilet and shower block himself.

When we first stayed there the facilities were basic. There was a loo and a shower but no doors on either. That had to wait until he had tracked some down. Each year would bring fresh improvements. However, everything was done as economically as possible so toilet basins and cisterns were not necessarily the same colour. Neither were sinks and pedestals and none of them were the same design. It was made up of whatever he had been able to get his hands on, cheaply.

Thus when you entered the shower block your eyes were assaulted by the most eclectic and colourful collection of sanitary equipment ever assembled. As we shall learn later, if it was in the Netherlands they would have made a museum out of it. All very clean and very serviceable but there were not two matching pieces in the entire ensemble.

The site was adjacent to the Stretton Hills bottled water plant. Indeed, you were allowed to help yourself to the water from a tap which had been thoughtfully placed at the front of the building. One of the things you may not know about such places is that the product isn't quite as natural as it sounds. The freshwater spring from which the water is taken is there sure enough, but to increase production nature is given a bit of a helping hand.

At various points along the flat valley floor you will notice small brick buildings. These house pumps, which pump the water from the ground up to the top of the hills, which then filters down through the rocks and back into the spring. The product therefore is natural enough but to get the volume required, let's just say they don't rely purely on rainwater.

My engineering caravan site owner and builder of psychedelic loos had figured out where the pumps needed to be placed to achieve the desired result. Not because he worked for the company, he'd done it just because he could. Some geniuses live very quiet lives indeed.

One of the best object lessons in man management I ever witnessed happened on a caravan site in Scotland. We were staying just up the road, on a CL, from a large static van holiday park. Among the attractions on the park was a fish and chip van, which was staffed, as was much of the park by students on summer vacation. One very fine and warm evening, Gill and I decided to get some fish and chips and walk down to the beach on the loch with them. Unfortunately, our thought wasn't as original as we had hoped, as so did everyone else on the holiday park and at more or less the same time. I guess there are not that many fine warm summer evenings on the west coast of Scotland when you can sit on the beach with fish and chips.

When we arrived at the fish and chip van, it was pandemonium. Five students, trying to feed what seemed like the five thousand with limited cooking facilities from a tiny converted caravan. The inexperienced catering team were panicing and one or two of them were visibly upset and frightened.

Into this chaos strode a young man of no more than twenty-five. I gathered later that he was the son of one of the owners. He immediately gave each one of the team very specific tasks. One person cooking chips, one cooking fish, one keeping stocks of raw material flowing, two serving customers. Then he organised the baying crowd into something like an orderly queue, dispensing charm, a smile and reassuring everyone that they would get fed.

He then went round each of the team telling them what a great job they were doing and lending a hand himself where anyone appeared to be struggling until they were back on top. He didn't stop repeating these tasks until the queue had disappeared. I used to use this example in some of the training I dispensed. I hope that he himself is now the successful owner of this business. From what I saw he deserves to be.

One of the great advantages of caravanning is

that you do get to go to places that you would not otherwise dream of visiting. At one point I thought of writing a chapter where I would list them all at you. However I dismissed the idea on the basis that, unless you are having trouble sleeping, you might not find it that interesting. What I have therefore done above is try to explain the attractions of going to some of the places you may not consider to be prime holiday locations.

If I was asked to summarise the main advantage of caravanning, I would say that you get to see some really nice places and you get to meet some really nice people. If I were asked to summarise the main disadvantages, I would say you get to see the odd not so nice place and you get to meet the odd grump but as Kanger wisely says to Roo, in the House at Pooh Corner. "Most people are nice if you take the trouble to get to know them."

ONE DOG AND
HIS CARAVAN

I have always been a reluctant dog owner. I guess I take the view that they stop you doing quite a lot of things. For example, what to do with them if you want to go to a restaurant or visit a tourist attraction where they are not allowed? However, I have also always been surrounded by enthusiastic dog lovers' right from my mum and dad through to my own family. In consequence I have always had a dog. Don't get me wrong it isn't all bad, and I have been very upset when our dogs have passed on so perhaps I love them better than I think. Dogs and caravans together present special challenges.

Back at home my mum and dad's dog was called Lassie. If you have been paying attention you will by now know that my parents named their children Janet and John and called the family dog

Lassie. If I have one criticism of them, it is that they had absolutely no imagination whatsoever when it came to names. Most parents agonise for months over what to call their offspring and even family pets. Mine it appears dispatched these decisions with alarming alacrity and I have always vaguely resented the fact that my sister and I are collectively a byword for something that is a bit simple. I'm only marginally surprised we were not called numbers one, two and three respectively. I suppose if I'd been Number One, it might have had a bit of a spacy Star Trek feel to it. I imagine my sister is eternally grateful not to be known as Number Two though. However I also know that she has never been especially fond of her name. She was called Janet as a child and shortened it to Jan as soon as she was old enough to exercise authority over the matter.

I was around sixteen years old, when after a long break from a succession of unimaginatively named dogs my parents and sister decided to rescue one from the dogs' home in Sheffield. Lassie was a Border Collie cum Jack Russell and around seven years old when we got her.

She actually got on with caravanning life very

well indeed. Dogs generally do, I think they like the feeling of the whole pack being cooped into a small space. She did have a habit of sleeping right by the door so that no one could enter or leave without her knowing about it. The downside, and believe me there is no such thing as the perfect dog, was that she hated travelling by car. From the moment the engine started she would howl, then howl some more and she would not stop howling until we arrived at our destination. No amount of comforting, fussing, stroking, playing, food, dog treats or threats of violence helped. I know we tried them all.

I have huge admiration for people who suffer from Tinnitus. We only had to put up with a poor impression of it for three or four hours at a stretch at the most. How you deal with it all the time including at night and retain even a shred of sanity is a mystery to me. My dad was completely deaf in one ear from being quite a young man and so received, we reckoned, half the dose but even he dreaded car journeys with her. The rest of us got her full volume howls in living stereo.

She loved to walk. Fortunately for her at the time so did we and so she got a lot of it. She climbed most of the fells in the Lake District including a precarious ascent of Jacobs Ladder with my dad pulling her up by her collar and me pushing her by her bottom. I somehow think I got the raw end of that deal.

She was a very good at always checking where you were. I think in the eight years or so that we had her she only ever got lost once and that was when she put her paw in a gamekeeper's snare and so was unable to move. The gamekeeper did eventually find her but not before she had spent a cold wet night outside

She was absolutely brilliant at finding mud and rolling in it. Even in the longest hottest summers when there was no mud left anywhere in the British Isles, Lassie would find a thick black smelly pool of it. This would usually be just towards the end of a walk when there was no convenient pond to chuck her in and clean her up. My mother who believes that cleanliness is way more important than godliness, which in her view doesn't even run it a poor second, used to despair. If you've ever slept in the confines of a caravan with a dog who thinks the most wondrous scent in the world is that produced from a good roll in fox pooh, you would have to concede that she does have a point.

Lassie lived for quite a while after I left home and continued to go caravanning with my parents. She departed this mortal coil shortly after they gave up caravanning for a few years. She must have missed it.

Gill is a serious and serial dog lover. She freely admits that she can't really cope with life without having a dog in it. Her own dog whilst she was growing up was Lady. Unlike Lassie she was quite a good traveller although I do gather that whoever travelled in the front passenger seat had to tuck their legs under their bum to leave the foot well available for canine transportation. Also unlike Lassie she was prone to going off on the odd adventure of her own and prone to returning in a less pristine state than she had been when she departed. Lady used to sleep on the floor of the caravan loo. Which was OK until someone wanted to use it as she would growl and defend her space with a determination last seen at the Siege of Mafeking. The whole family must have had to develop bladders like horses.

Gill and I's first family dog was another seven-year-old rescue case. He came with the name "Bol"

I can only speculate as to how this came about. Maybe his original owners had the surname Locke or Locking and they thought it hilarious. Possibly his original kennel club name was something like Testicles out of Scrotum. This last suggestion is unlikely, a dog less likely to have a kennel club name would be difficult to find.

In any event we concluded that shouting "Bol" across a field at regular intervals would one day inevitably get one of us beaten up or arrested, so we changed the last letter and Bob's your dog. He didn't seem to mind and got used to it quite quickly.

Bob's downside, and we were warned about this when we got him, was that he would scrap with anything. He was the ear biting Mike Tyson of the canine world. Maybe it was his name, to paraphrase Johnny Cash, "Life Ain't Easy for Dog Named Bol" Notwithstanding this we had him separated from them and I am pleased to report that after a year or so he did improve.

On the upside he was very gentle with children and very protective of my daughter who came along shortly after we got him. Gill would leave the pram outside a shop with the baby in it. If anyone looked in the pram Bob would start a low warning growl which got more threatening if they didn't back off. Someone would have to have been very brave indeed to touch her. Bob lived to be fourteen and died the year before we got our first caravan, so technically he shouldn't be included in this chapter but it felt wrong somehow to just airbrush him from history.

Our first ever puppy was another rescue dog called Spot. Oh dear! I can hear my mother muttering something about pots kettles and black, so here is the case for the defence. Our children named him, they were very into a character called Spot the Dog created by Eric Hill at the time and as a small puppy he did actually have a spot. This turned into more of a Blodge as he got older, but you can't expect a four-year-old to predict that. My mother probably has some equally lame excuse for her un-inspiring choice of names.

Spot was a pedigree Heinz 57 found in a carrier bag, in a shop doorway, on the streets of Birken-head, so even having me as an owner represented a big success in terms of social mobility. He was a fantastic family dog, endlessly patient with young children, who must at times have made his life hell, but if they did he never showed it. Spot loved travelling and loved caravanning. He always slept in the tiny space under the front bed. He persisted in this habit all his life even when he was quite old, rheumatism had overtaken him, and frankly he should have known better. Therefore, in later life, he spent the first twenty minutes each morning performing various physiotherapy exercises to get all his bits working.

Years ago, to make up the front bed in a caravan you folded the leg down on the dining table, popped it on some ledges between the two front settees, put the rear bolster cushions on top of it, slept on it and then wondered why you woke up with a bad back. These days there is a nice neat row of slats that pulls out to create a rather more comfortable and much better ventilated slatted bed such as you might buy in Ikea.

Spot was also the only dog I have had with whom you could successfully cycle. He would run along on a lead at the side of you and provided you accommodated him by not going too fast he would accommodate you by matching your pace. His main distinguishing feature was a huge bushy tail out of all proportion to the rest of him. When he was happy, which was most of the time, he would arch it round so that it touched his back. The whole thing looked like a Tina Turner hair do.

I don't remember him ever running off, perhaps having lived on the streets of Merseyside once, he wasn't anxious to repeat the experience. I've been trying to think of Spot's downside, he must have had one, but if so I can't remember it. His final holiday was in Milton Keynes, but by this time he was seventeen years old and I couldn't get him to walk to the end of the drive of the site, so shortly after we returned home I took him to the vets. I cried when he died.

Enter Darwin. Again my daughter chose this name, although she was by now thirteen years old and there really is no excuse. It wasn't even meant as a tribute to the man who was arguably Britain's greatest ever scientist, a fact of which I think she is still only dimly aware.

I was working away at the time and I returned home on the Friday to find out I was once again a dog owner with yet another pre-named dog. My daughter has never given me an adequate explanation for the name. Gill was just so pleased to have a new dog that she would have agreed to anything so I suppose on reflection it could have been much worse.

Gill and the now fairly grown up children had been out to Wales and gotten the dog from a farm. As people who know about these things will tell you, this is about the worst way possible to get a new puppy. Why? Some of the more disreputable sheep farmers will make a bitch have fifty or sixty puppies in the hope of getting one decent sheep dog. The overwhelming majority of them of course are not wanted, they can often be the result of brother mated with sister, but hey if they can charge you £80 to a £100 for one then there's even a profit in failure. More recently it has become illegal to either buy or sell a puppy in this way.

What we got was a much overbred, very highly strung and very nervy, border collie. He was lucky in that he didn't have to cope with young children poking and prodding him and that Gill loved him to bits and invested hours of time and patience in him that I would never have had. He was never comfortable around other dogs and was a bit over protective of Gill, but she did succeed, and it is Gill that must take all the credit here, in making, against all the odds, a very nice dog out of him.

He was inexhaustible, I took him on some twenty mile hikes, during which he must have covered three times that distance and yet at the end of it he would still be bringing me sticks to throw for him. To watch him run or jump was like poetry. Every muscle in his body working in perfect harmony as he charged across a field, paws never leaving the ground by more than an inch, in hot pursuit of say a rabbit and boy could he jump. If you threw a hard ball high in the air, he would catch it on the first bounce, sometimes leaping over two metres in the air to do so and only rarely did he miss. He would happily spend hours chasing balls.

The downside of this was that he was completely indiscriminate in what he chased. Rabbits, birds, bikes, tractors, lorries and cars, it was frightening. I have a collection of Ordnance Survey maps covering most of the country just so that we could work out when we were approaching a road before he did. We were sure that in the end it would be chasing something that ended his life. In the end it was liver disease. Poor chap never had a drink in his life either so far as I am aware.

He was the first and to date only dog we have ever taken abroad with us. This wasn't that difficult whilst we were members of the EU. You simply got him a passport in which your vet certified he was vaccinated against Rabies and one or two other less unpleasant diseases. You popped him through a scanner at the port, an official would check the chip number matched the passport and that was it. It may be trickier in the future.

He was absolutely rubbish at cycling, after three or four unexpected, alarming, but no doubt spectacular dismounts from a spectator's viewpoint, I gave up. He made up for it by not complaining if I left him at the caravan so long as I took him good walk before and after.

One thing you could not leave Darwin in the caravan for, or anywhere else for that matter was a Thunderstorm. He was absolutely terrified. As you might guess you do feel a little closer to nature in a caravan than you would in a house, and as many of you will know, some of the thunderstorms you get on the continental land mass are spectacular.

We tried everything, plug in contraptions that are supposed to release a calming odour by heating fragrant oils. Thunder coats that are supposed to relax the dog by acting on pressure points. Tablets that were meant to calm him, nothing worked. Neighbours would complain as they would think we had left him outside, such was the volume of his panicked barking, it nearly got us chucked off a site once. He never got over it.

We are very fortunate in the UK in that there are very few things in our natural environment that will either kill or cause you serious injury, the odd adder perhaps, but that really is about it. One of the downsides of the Dutch summer is that in addition to the wild boar that roam the forests freely, there are some fairly nasty bugs out there. The oak procession caterpillar may sound innocuous enough, but get stung by their spines and you need to get to hospital pretty quickly. They also have a preponderance of sheep ticks which potentially carry Lyme's Disease. Again if you get treatment pretty quickly you will be OK but the problem with ticks is that you don't always know that you have been bitten until it's too late.

One year Gill presented me with what looked like two garters, the kind of thing gentlemen use to keep their socks up. Once installed, she advised me, they repel ticks and all other insects that are likely to look for a free lunch off your body. Even so they looked like something I used to wear when I was a boy scout. It was my job to walk Darwin, so I did worry about these things.

A tick is a tiny balloon shaped insect, closely related to a spider, which crawls up short trees and tall grass. When it detects your legs pass by, it swings, Tarzan like, and attaches itself to you. It then burrows a hole in your leg into which it inserts the narrow end of its balloon shaped body. It then proceeds to suck blood, thus inflating said balloon to the size of a large peanut. A tick's saliva contains an anaesthetic so you feel nothing, at least initially.

They can be extracted using a small tool which looks like one end of a tiny claw hammer. However, if you are a bit of a wimp like me, the pain is excruciating and not to be endured without a good slug of a very large whisky first.

As noted earlier they carry the risk of infecting you with Lyme's Disease. This amongst other things causes memory loss, extreme laziness and paranoia. Gill thinks I may already have it, but Just in case I haven't, she presented me with the garters. I walk the dog, through the woods and laugh in the face of the omnipresent yet unseen danger.

Reading the instructions on my new ankle garters informed me that they contain millions of balls and they work by the unlikely sounding expedient of releasing a vague smell, harmless and undetectable to humans, but if you are a tick, then it is equivalent of the four horsemen of the apocalypse. Still I do have to admit that I never picked up a tick whilst wearing them. Darwin on the other hand was less fortunate and over a two-week period I extracted at least twenty of the little blighters using the aforementioned claw hammer. He was actually a very decent chap about letting me remove them and far more stoical about the pain than I would have been.

If you imagine that Darwin had only say ten percent of my body mass, he was, after all only a small border collie, then from his point of view someone removing an item the size of say a pear from your head, or inside your thigh, or even more shockingly your penis, must be a tad disconcerting to say the least. Yet, he uncomplainingly let me perform my surgery without so much as a whimper. True Dunkirk spirit. I think the ticks may even have done me a bit of a favour. In Gill's eyes at least I became something of a superhero, rooting out all ticks wherever they may be. She became my sort of Lois Lane swooning over her fearless man. I maybe overegging the pudding a bit here but the bit about her admiration for my tick removal skills I stand by.

Our current canine is a Sprocker Spaniel. He is probably the nicest natured dog we have ever owned, in that he just wants to play with everyone, big dogs, little dogs, big people, little people, he just wants to play. He is also by far and away the most expensive dog we have ever owned, I'm not telling you what we paid for him, it upsets me too much. He is called Bailey, we thought we were being original by naming him after the caravan. However, we were in a dog friendly café one day as were predictably another three dogs, every single one of them called Bailey. My confidence in my capacity for original thought took a severe knock that day.

Bailey hasn't done a lot of caravanning yet. A little bit around Shropshire and Stafford when my daughter was giving birth to our fourth grandchild, but that has been it. His early life included the Corona virus lockdown. I concluded that he was quite happy with the status quo. Long walks from home, with no need to get in a car and the operation to separate him from his testicles was cancelled indefinitely. I am sure I used to periodically catch him looking at me with an expression that said, "What's not to like about this?"

Bailey is something of a babe magnet. He wears that lugubrious expression cultivated by spaniels everywhere which says, "My life is awful and he doesn't feed me you know, can I go with you?" Pretty young girls seem particularly vulnerable at falling for this line. None of it is true of course, but that doesn't matter. The way he spins it, they swallow it hook line and sinker every single time. They hug him, kiss him, allow him to paw them in the most inappropriate way and they don't even mind, in fact they love it. They regard me with a look of pure hatred which says "How could you, you cruel man?" I of course am expected to take the opprobrium without comment. I suspect any appeal on my part would fall upon deaf ears anyway.

If there are sufficient attractive females around, he will peddle this tale several times in the course of just one walk. If he were human he would be considered a philanderer, a cad and a bounder of the sort that mothers issue stern warnings about to their daughters. I sometimes tell him this as we eventually walk away from some beautiful young woman whose heart he has just broken. He simply looks at me with puzzled bemusement and say's "What moi?" in a hurt tone of voice. We move on to his next conquest and he gets away with it.

I bought him a carriage which I drag along behind the bike. It is covered so he is protected from the elements, but you can unzip a canvas trap door in the roof so he can stick his head out and complain to anyone who happens to be about with a look that says, "Have you seen how cruelly he treats me. I am the product of hundreds of years of careful breading and he treats me like a caravan."

The scariest experience I ever had with a dog was not my own dog. We were in the Netherlands near a town called Heino. In the morning I would usually cycle down to the nearest village and get fresh bread for breakfast. On my return journey I noticed a guy stood in his garden with a truly enormous dog. One of those that you sometimes see menacingly patrolling behind a reassuringly sturdy security fence. I paid no heed. That was until I had just passed the entrance to the garden. At that point came a ferocious bark followed by galloping paws and increasingly desperate cries of "Uno, Uno" from the man in his garden which Uno showed no signs obeying. I don't know what the world record for speed cycling is, but I reckon I came pretty close to smashing it that day. Uno did eventually give up the chase, but for the remainder of the holiday I found a different route to the bakery.

Some of you may be thinking that the fact we have always had dogs is the reason we have chosen caravan holidays and that we have never had the pleasure of being waited on hand and foot in an Hotel. Well you would be wrong, I spent the last twenty-five years of my career more or less living in hotels. The Holiday Inn at Milton Keynes once gave me a bottle of bubbly in honour of my one hundredth check in, which probably means I spent between three and four hundred nights there alone, but I stayed in a lot of hotels up and down the country. I was very lucky and there are few major towns and cities in the UK that I haven't visited at one time or another. Best Hotel? I don't know, possibly The Lygon Arms at Broadway or

The Old Hall at Sutton Coldfield but I stayed in some crackers. Worst Hotel? Well that would be unfair as it's a while ago now and I don't want to get sued. I did stay in the odd shocker but not often. One claimed that I was sleeping in the same bedroom as Charles Dickens had done. If I was, and I can only judge from the smell, either it hadn't been serviced since or his rotting corpse was still in it.

Hotel managers were usually fairly pleased to see me, not least because I was often booking their facilities to run training courses and bringing with me between ten or fifteen other guests. Thanks to their gratitude and rewards programmes Gill and I also got to stay in some very nice hotels together.

Working away so much sometimes caused a few headaches when it came to getting away in the caravan. On one occasion, just before our main summer holiday, I was working in Milton Keynes all week which would have meant I had to get back home to The Wirral on the Friday and then immediately set back off south for the Channel Tunnel. To save the planet and reduce our carbon footprint, Gill towed the caravan down to Milton Keynes and we started the holiday from there.

My part of the bargain was to make sure I got the Euros we would need. When you are caravanning you tend to need to carry more cash. Small caravan sites rarely take credit cards and in the early days banks charged you a fortune to use cash dispensers abroad. I've since found better ways of solving this problem but back then I calculated we would need around two thousand Euros which I was to get from the Post Office. On the Thursday I duly nipped out at lunchtime, got the cash and carried it around with me for the rest of the day.

On the Thursday evening I went to Milton Keynes excellent theatre with some colleagues and so left the Euros in the combination lock safe in my hotel room. I returned some hours later and it must be admitted having had a few drinks, over the course of what had been a very pleasant evening.

Now, have you ever done something when you have had a drink that seemed perfectly logical to you at the time but in the cold light of day doesn't really stand up to scrutiny? If you have you may feel a pang of empathy for what happens next. If not you will just think "Idiot" Either way it's OK, I'm used to it.

I was really worried that I would leave the

hotel the following morning and forget to take the Euros, currently languishing in the safe, so I opened it, took out the money and placed it in my shoes. "Can't forget my shoes", I reasoned. I then; and I know not to this day why I did this, placed the shoes in the safe and re-locked it. I went to sleep safe in the knowledge that my cash and my shoes were secure.

The following morning, I woke up, performed all my usual ablutions, finished packing and searched for my shoes. I started looking in all the likely places that they could possibly be, wardrobe, by the door, under the bed. Then with increasing panic I looked in all the unlikely places that they could not possibly be. On top of the wardrobe, in the bin, in the mini bar, eventually I remembered the safe. Breathing a sigh of relief, I keyed in the code. "Error" proclaimed the electronic display on the front of the safe in very smug red letters. I tried again and again. It is said that repeating the same behaviour and expecting a different result is one definition of madness. Short of dropping its trousers and pulling moonies at me the safe could not have been more self-satisfied or uncooperative.

Eventually I rang reception. This is Friday morning when the world and his wife are all checking out so no one is answering the phone. I gave up and padded down to reception in my stockinged feet. Several people in the queue surveyed my feet and looked at me strangely. You could see the look on their faces, they almost had think balloons above their heads which said: "I wonder if I should tell him he's forgotten something?" All of them thought better of it and simply smiled. I smiled back weakly.

At the front of the queue I explained my predicament and the very helpful receptionist, who did a pretty good display of empathy, explained that someone would come to help me. I returned to the sanctity of my room and shortly after a young woman in hotel uniform arrived clutching what looked like a cross between a stethoscope and a blood pressure machine.

She attached wires to hitherto unseen plugs on the safe door and pressed various buttons. After various buzzes and beeps the safe door sprung open releasing the powerful odour of my imprisoned shoes. The girl visibly recoiled. When she had recovered herself she regarded me with a quizzical look. "Very expensive shoes" I offered, but I could tell she wasn't convinced. I have never used a hotel safe since.

My other embarrassing hotel experience was actually work related, but you might be beginning to see why, on the whole, I find caravanning a more relaxing way to spend my leisure time.

On this occasion I was heading to Leeds on the M62 one Sunday evening for an early start on the Monday. As I was passing Manchester I thought I could really do with the loo. Now for the avoidance of doubt later in this story I should clarify that we are talking about a number two here. Not particularly liking the Birch service area, West of Manchester I carried on safe in the knowledge that Hartshead Moor with its much more upmarket feel was a mere twenty minutes or so further up the motorway. Unfortunately, I wasn't really paying attention when I got to the slip road into the service area and I shot past it.

Never mind I thought, though by this time I was feeling distinctly uncomfortable, I can wait till I get to the hotel, just! Now I had never stopped at the Marriott Hotel in central Leeds before. Those of you who know it will also know that it isn't that easy to find, situated as it is at the heart of Leeds' impenetrable one-way system.

I eventually drew up outside the main entrance, by now the beads of sweat were standing out on my forehead. A concierge shot out and admonished me. "You can't park there; you can't park there." He shouted. My pleas for mercy went unacknowledged. "You have to go in the NCP in Boar Lane" I sought urgent directions and set off again this time with my right foot operating the brake and my left the clutch and accelerator.

It wasn't until I got near the top floor that I found a parking space. I grabbed my bags, ran to the lift and jabbed urgently on the button. The lift is turned off on a Sunday, so I ran and I do mean ran down the stairs and across the precinct. I arrived at reception, explained I had a reservation and more or less asked them to make it snappy. Why I didn't just find the loos in the public area of the hotel I don't know, but you don't always think logically under pressure and I couldn't remember feeling under this much pressure for a long time.

The receptionist gave me my credit card style room key and pointed to the lifts. "Room 525" she loftily declared. After yet more urgent jabbing of the lift call button it eventually arrived. I entered and the lift ascended at an agonisingly slow rate to the fifth floor. I shot out and sprinted down the corridor, from my knees downward anyway. At the entrance to my room I pushed the key into the slot and the door opened just under the pressure of this movement. I didn't give it any thought at the time. I entered, tossed my bags to the right ran through the bathroom door to the left, dropped my trousers and made it with less than a second to spare.

If there is a better feeling in the world, I have yet to encounter it. I did what by this time simply had to be done, washed my hands and feeling more relaxed than I had for some considerable time opened the door. It was then I came face to face with a tall broadly set Scotsman.

He simply said "This is my room."

I drew the key card from my pocket. "No, 525" I countered.

"This is 523, that's next door" he replied.

"Oh dear I'm sorry about that" I responded, even then aware of the total inadequacy of my apology in the light of what I had just done.

Sensing that a more thorough explanation might merely inflame the situation I left it at that. Actually under the circumstances he was very nice about it. I apologised again picked up my bags and beat a hasty retreat and fervently hoped the odour I had left him with would do the same. Fortunately, I did not bump in to my neighbour again for the remainder of my stay.

There are some people who really shouldn't stop in hotels and I'm probably one of them. You would think that after all the time I've spent in such establishments I'd be better at it but I'm not, so as I said at the start caravans are probably a better option for me.

LIFE ON EASY STREET

When I first started work at the tender age of eighteen, I had no thought of retirement. I don't suppose many of us do. I had no hobbies or interests outside of work, and I therefore flung myself into it with great gusto. Over anxious to please and it has to be said a somewhat gauche youth my first venture into the world of work was an abject failure and unmitigated disaster, luckily so as things turned out. My first employer, as I mentioned briefly in an earlier chapter, was British Home Stores. Of course had I been more successful I might well have spent the next forty years working for them and retired just in time to see what would have been a non-contributory final salary pension scheme vanish quicker than you can say Philip Green.

The first and only store I worked at was in Preston. This was also incidentally the first time I left home. The manager hated me with a passion I had hitherto not experienced. I think it was only partially personal, he didn't seem to like anyone very much. It may seem strange now but BHS in those days was considered to have the finest management training programme in the industry. In some respects it was supposedly better than the hallowed Marks & Spencer who were at the time the most successful retailer that the UK had ever seen.

I remember my first day getting off the train from Sheffield, I had left home at around 5:00 a.m. to catch the early train to Manchester. In those days to get to Preston you had first to go to Manchester Piccadilly and then walk across the city to Victoria Station, so it was quite a tortuous journey. I walked up the main street in Preston, which was where the mighty BHS had for reasons best known to itself deemed that I should be employed. I arrived in the store shortly after 9:00 a.m. and made myself known.

The store manager a diminutive unsmiling man of I suppose thirty five-ish, but seemed much older to me at the time, was summonsed. He looked at me with barely concealed disappointment, though to this day I don't really know why and told me to follow him. He admonished me for the time of my arrival even though my appointment letter stated I should arrive by 9:30.

Things went downhill from there and didn't really improve until I announced my departure some eight months later. Actually they didn't improve much then either. Still at least I always knew where I stood with him - On the wrong side.

I spent the ensuing months being trained by moving around the various different departments spending several weeks in each. From warehouse to back office to shop floor to food preparation area to restaurant, I did the lot. The only common feature was each department manager's ability to mirror the intense dislike of the store manager towards me. The exception was the food prep area, the ladies here including the manager were all without exception absolutely lovely. Moreover, I learned to butcher a pig. Not a skill I have needed since but if you ever need a pig converting into rashers of bacon and gammon joints then I'm your man.

To be fair, as I say, I was a rather gauche youth

and younger than most management trainees recruited by BHS at the time. I lacked any life experience, came from Yorkshire and probably wasn't very likeable. I also found, with the notable exception of carving up pigs, that it was the most crushingly boring and miserable experience of my life either before or since.

What I learned, apart from knowing how to create perfectly sliced bacon, was that if you come across someone who doesn't like you, there is very little you can do about it, unless you can uncover their reason. At the time I lacked the skills to do this.

Like everyone else I had some Saturday jobs while I was at school, my first was working as a kitchen porter in House of Fraser's rather up-market restaurant and what a fantastic job it was too. OK cleaning out the stock-pot wasn't great and you came home stinking of stale food but there were compensations. The pastry chef used to give me a cake to have with my lunch, the girl on the friar would give me a portion of chips, the barmaid would give me a beer when I went to clear her empties. I was only fifteen at the time and like all fifteen year old boys I could eat for England.

I learnt a couple of things from this job too. Firstly, no matter how bad a meal is never ever send it back and secondly, never ever be rude to anyone serving you food. I saw first-hand what happened to some food backstage if a customer upset chef or the waitresses. I'll not trouble you with the gory details, just don't do it. I'm sure fifty years on these things would never happen now, but I still wouldn't take the risk if I were you.

My second Saturday job was working for Boots the Chemist in their photographic department. I absolutely loved this job and it was on this basis that I thought I might have an aptitude for retail management. I applied to Marks & Spencer, who wisely declined my offer to improve their already then exulted position, and to BHS. As we have established I was wrong about being any good at retail management but what I did have aptitude for was talking to people, selling them expensive cameras and photographic equipment.

This skill transferred surprisingly well into the last job I ever applied for, that of a management trainee with the Leeds Permanent Building Society. After that I never changed employer again though employers changed me quite a few times.

The Leeds was taken over by the Halifax, which was merged with the Bank of Scotland, which was taken over by Lloyds Bank.

Forty years after I started work for the Leeds the mighty Lloyds Banking Group were looking for some redundancies. I'd never made any secret of the fact that I'd always planned to retire at sixty and being fifty-eight at the time I thought "two year's money for not doing two year's work? They'll never go for that." But I ticked the voluntary redundancy box anyway. Fortunately for me banks are not as good at mathematics as you would think they might be, although this might not come as a surprise to some readers. In September 2016 they dispensed with my services leaving me with the wherewithal to buy a spanking brand new caravan and the income to go and enjoy my hobby on a full time basis.

All of the above is a long winded introduction to what you can do when you don't have the inconvenience of work to worry about. For each of the years since we retired Gill and I have spent more nights away in our caravan than we have spent at home. For reasons that I am sure will eventually be extensively documented elsewhere we did not achieve that feat in 2020.

Caravans had undergone yet another revolution since we had last replaced ours. All the caravans my parents had and indeed the ones I have owned up to 2016 were essentially wooden frames with sheets of aluminium riveted to them. The whole thing was made waterproof with liberal amounts of mastic around the joints. The problem with this method of construction is that mastic over the years hardens and becomes brittle. Once it is brittle it can fall out. It is also easy to leave gaps in it where water can ingress. Once water penetrates the wooden frame it will start to rot. Thus it used to be very common for older caravans and even some newer ones to literally fall apart. Some manufacturers were notoriously unsympathetic towards customers whose pride and joy was dropping to pieces. Most caravans nowadays are constructed on aluminium or advanced plastic frames with seamless bonded panels. I'm not an expert but the problem of damp caravans seems to have virtually disappeared.

Our new caravan came with roof mounted solar panels so you now had off grid electricity. It has a fixed bed with a proper mattress so no more con verting bench seats to bed before you could sleep. It has built in music systems, television point and USB sockets abound everywhere you look.

Modern caravans have built in central heating systems, many of which can be controlled from an app on your phone. They also have high levels of insulation and are therefore surprisingly snug in the winter. There are however one or two draw backs to winter caravanning, one of which is the inconvenience of the convenience water cistern being frozen. Another is remembering to bring the fresh water tank inside the caravan on cold nights and making sure you've filled it up before retiring. Failure to do so not only means you can't get a shower in the morning, even a cup of tea must wait until you've managed to thaw out the forty litre block of ice attached to the side of your van by an equally frozen submersible pump. The standpipe water tap on the site is also likely to be frozen.

However, winter caravanning has its compensations. There are some places which are especially beautiful to see on bright crisp winter mornings. Granted, there are also some mornings when you can't see anything at all. The mountains of North

Wales or the Cheshire Plains or the Shropshire Hills are all fairly close by for us. In winter when you perhaps don't want to tow your van too far you can have them all to yourself.

Another advantage is the number of places where you can eat and drink really cheaply as country pubs and other establishments make all sorts of offers to tempt you in, to survive after most tourists have gone home. An increasing number of caravan sites, especially Certificated Locations, remain open for the full twelve months. Finding somewhere to stay isn't a problem and on smaller sites you will either have the place to yourself or share the space with perhaps one other unit.

Of course the real advantage of retirement is that you are no longer restricted to a stay of two weeks, you can go for as long as you want. There are some practical limitations, like how long you can leave your house uninhabited before your insurance company starts getting twitchy. Your mobile phone stops working after you have been out of the country for two months. It's also probably wise to periodically remind your children what you look like. We have so far chosen to spend the majority of our longer stays back in our much beloved Netherlands. Why? Well, we have acquired friends over there and we would miss seeing them.

Jan and Tineke, whom we met back in chapter four allow us to leave our caravan with them whilst we return to the UK for a few weeks. We cycle a lot and there is no better place in the world for this, although Milton Keynes does run it a close second. I have learned to speak Dutch passably well, although my pronunciation and grammar still causes the natives great amusement. We find the pace of life in rural Netherlands very relaxed. I sometimes think one of changes I have noticed in the UK in recent years is people's capacity to get very angry over things that on the face of it don't seem that important. In this regard the Netherlands seem to be behind us. I hope they remain so forever.

We like the Dutch and they seem to like us. There is a bond between us partly but not exclusively formed in war. If you visit Oosterbeek near Arnhem during May or September, every house and I do mean every house, will have the maroon and pale blue flag of the 4th Parachute Brigade hung from a pole at the front of the house to commemorate Operation Market Garden. I have had

Dutchman shake my hand and thank me for their liberation even though I obviously wouldn't even have been a twinkle in my father's eye at the time. Strangely this has never ever happened to me in France.

Market Garden was the failed allied operation launched in September 1944 to try and capture the bridges over the Rhine and end the war by Christmas that year. The historic events are captured fairly accurately in the film "A Bridge Too Far" if you are interested. If you visit the excellent museum at Oosterbeek, outside you will find a stone that bares this inscription.

TO THE PEOPLE OF GELDERLAND

50 years ago British and Polish airborne soldiers fought here against overwhelming odds to open the way into Germany and bring the war to an early end. Instead we brought death and destruction for which you have never blamed us.

This stone marks our admiration for your great courage, remembering especially the women who tended our wounded. In the long winter that followed your families risked death by hiding Allied soldiers and airmen, while members of the resist-

ance helped many to safety.

You took us into your homes as fugitives and friends, we took you forever into our hearts. This strong bond will continue long after we are all gone.

1944 SEPTEMBER 1994

For some reason I can't explain it always brings a tear to my eye. Perhaps it is because it so perfectly encapsulates that bond which exists between the British and the Dutch.

They much lament our leaving the EU because as semi-reluctant Europeans themselves, they saw us as an ally in preventing some of the worse carve ups between the French and Germans often at the expense of smaller countries like the Netherlands.

We have a very similar sense of humour. Back at the museum in Oosterbeek there is a section of internal wall from the original building that has been preserved. All of the explanatory notices in the museum are written first in Dutch, second in English and third in German. This particular piece of wall has been preserved because on it one of the Tommie's has kept record of the number of Germans he killed by scrawling a swastika for each one. Underneath he added "Fuck the Gerrys – never surrender". The explanatory note at the side translates this First into Dutch, secondly if unnecessarily into English and third into German. Suffice it say, as a Brit you can always be assured of a warm welcome in the Netherlands.

The Dutch are very fond of museums they have hundreds and hundreds of them catering to every taste and some of them are not very tasteful at all. I've never been, honestly, but in Amsterdam there is a museum of sex and erotica. Among the more unusual offerings are: a writing machine museum, baking museum, Drugs museum, a museum of self-playing musical instruments, a museum of microbes, though to be fair it was a Dutchman that invented the microscope. The point is that if you can have a museum about it, they've probably got one.

The area of engineering in which the Dutch truly excel is water management. It has been said that God created the world but the Dutch created the Netherlands and when you look at some of the structures they have built you can see what a monumental achievement it was. There are whole tracts of agricultural land, towns and cities that are below sea level and should by rights be under several metres of water. When you look at the infrastructure they have built to move water around, keep it where it is, stop it from damaging things, use it where it's needed and keep it away from where it's not needed, it is remarkable. Massive dykes that extend for miles, 20 miles in one case. Huge locks to make it navigable and gigantic pumps to move it around. There is of course a museum about water management full of interesting facts and artefacts about the Netherlands fight with the sea. Probably several.

A few years ago when the Somerset Levels experienced severe flooding, the Dutch apparently lent us some pumping equipment basically to get water off the plain and back into the river. The British engineers who installed them, started them up and thought they would need to run them for a couple of days. After two hours they noticed the pumps were making a strange noise. When they looked down at what was previously a lake, the area was completely dry. One of the solutions proposed by the Netherlands to rising sea levels is to build a 475 kilometre dam across the North Sea from Scotland to Norway. I don't doubt for a second that they could do it. No one beats the Dutch when it comes to water management.

The rest of Europe ascribes to the Dutch the qualities we English ascribe to Scotsmen or Yorkshiremen by giving them a reputation for being careful with their money. Personally I have always found them very generous so I suspect the claim doesn't stand up to any more scrutiny than the idea that all the mean people live in the North of the British Isles. I do however think I know why they have acquired this tag.

They never seem to throw anything away. If they no longer have need of an item they will pop it at the end of the drive, complete with a price tag, and offer it for consideration to passers-by. Old bicycles, old ironing boards, old prams, old toys, old tools, in fact old anything. The thing is that most of it is absolute junk of the type that you can find on any household waste disposal site in the UK and the price tags are mostly, well, optimistic to say the least.

In a refinement of this recycling technique, most towns and villages will periodically hold a Rommel Market, literally a Roman Market, in the town centre and practically any junk that happens to be lying around is for sale.

The thing is that quite a lot of what is on offer doesn't even work. I have seen burnt lampshades, cracked pots, glasses with broken stems, broken spanners, half a pair of scissors; all lovingly priced with a small white card attached. I have no idea who buys it. I have watched these markets for hours and never seen anyone actually part with any cash, but they are very popular.

Every town or village that is holding a Rommel market will proudly announce the fact weeks in advance with posters in every bar and café and digital display boards at the entrance to the town. If vendors are unable to sell their wares they are pretty laid back about it, they just pack it up and come back the next month and try their luck again until either it does sell or they die, whichever happens first.

The Dutch are pretty laid back about most things really. I have seen mechanics at petrol stations leant up against the pumps smoking a fag. I once said to one such individual that it wouldn't be allowed in England. "If happens it happens" he replied. The fact that half the village would be blown to kingdom come with him did not seem to be of great concern. Maybe it was something stronger than tobacco he was smoking.

I mentioned back in Chapter four, we are very fortunate in that when we go to the Netherlands we are able to stay in the garden of our friend's home. This is on the edge of the small town of Elspeet and therefore gives us access to both the facilities in the town and the extensive Fietsnetwork or cycle tracks.

The only slightly hairy bit of arriving at Jan and Tineke's place is getting the caravan to the bottom of the garden. To do this I have to negotiate a path between a line of oak trees and one of the holiday homes with less clearance than afforded by the hoistable car deck of a North Sea Ferry.

Every year, I say it can't be done and I plead with Jan to be allowed to do this with my motor mover. That's the thing that turns a caravan into a giant remote control toy, and every year he insists that I tow it down the path. He the cool-headed Dutchman issuing very precise guidance, me the profusely sweating Englishman squeezing the entire rig past the roof gables of one of his properties, a few centimetres at a time, with about an inch to spare and clutch screaming for mercy. Every year he is right and I am wrong.

We always celebrate this minor achievement with an English beer. I bring a selection of English beers with me for him to try and most afternoons we will sit down and share one together. Taking beer to the Netherlands is a bit like taking coals to Newcastle, but we Brits brew very different beers. Jan is always polite when he samples my beer, but sometimes I do catch him grimacing, he hasn't actually spluttered one out yet, but sometimes I think it's been a close run thing. I have however established that he does like Sharp's Atlantic Pale Ale. The arrival ceremony is generally closely observed by Jan's gardener Johan who occupies one of the former holiday homes. I say gardener but I have never actually seen him do any gardening.

Johan's story is quite a sad one. For many years he looked after his mother who was very sick. When she died he was unceremoniously turfed off the family farm by his brother who wanted to sell it. Johan ended up renting, though I don't think much rent is involved, for one of the ever charitable Jan's former holiday homes.

There he finds solace in the bottom of a beer can, quite a few beer cans actually. If you have an image that all the Dutch are clean, well that is generally true, but Johan is the exception that proves that rule. Let's just say that Johan and soap are not well acquainted, hardly on speaking terms in fact.

His home which was once a pleasant, if small, brick and timber holiday house has over time been turned into something that is host to so many bugs and germs, I suspect that some of them are probably banned under the terms of the Geneva Convention. I doubt anyone not wearing a chemical warfare suit could venture in there now and expect to live. It is in short, like its occupant, filthy. Due to an illness many years ago Jan has no sense of smell, the rest of us are not so fortunate.

Johan is however very entertaining. One-day Gill and I were doing some weeding for Jan, Johan joined us briefly to inform us that it was "Pinkster-dag" a religious public holiday in the Netherlands (we would call it Pentecost). He took a long swig from his can of beer which contains 15% proof of gut rotting lager and informed us that we should not be working on such an important religious day. Before this moment Johan had never struck me as a particularly devout man. He then staggered off announcing that he must work and water the garden. I thought of pointing out the inconsistency between this and his previous statement, but thought better of it. He then slumped into a garden chair, can of beer in one hand and a hose pipe in the other pointed vaguely in the direction of a flower bed. The only times I saw him move for the remainder of the afternoon, was to keep replenishing his beer.

On another occasion I found Johan eating his dinner in the garden. The dinner was croquet potatoes. The Dutch are very fond of these and they are available in a variety of flavours from most snack bars and cafes. The problem was that he was finding it extremely difficult to locate precisely where his mouth was. He had been successful at least once, as he had bitten the end off. However, since then he had stabbed himself several times in the face with the now soggy snack leaving potato imprints across his chin both cheeks and intriguingly, during what must have been a particularly spectacular failure, his forehead. The whole effect reminded me of something I once watched Tony Hart do on Vision-On with paint and foam rubber cut into various shapes.

One rather disconcerting event concerning Johan

happened a few years ago, but before I get to that you need to know that Gill wasn't exactly at the back of the queue when they handed out boobs. In consequence she sometimes attracts unsought, but nonetheless ardent admirers who have conversations with her chest.

One of the most ardent and most unsought of these is Johan. Gill had been doing some washing that included one of her bras which she hung on the rotary clothes drier whilst we went out cycling. On our return some hours later she took in the now dry washing. This was when she noticed that the supporting ironwork, by which I mean the underwires of the cups had been crushed and twisted out of shape. The most likely perpetrator of this wanton act of vandalism would appear to be Johan. Whilst we have no proof, he seems to be the one that had both motive and most certainly opportunity.

As noted earlier Johan is not the cleanest of individuals. I could tell that the thought of his tobacco stained beer soaked fingers snaking their way through her underwear was just too much for Gill. Had there been a handy branch of Bravissimo within say a three hundred mile radius the offending item would have been committed to the bin or more likely burnt and we would have been off to procure a replacement. However, such a thing does not exist in Northern Europe and we had another five weeks holiday to go. So reluctantly, I bent the wires back into shape as best I could, using another bra as a template. Gill washed and re-washed it and hung it out, this time with a 24/7 armed guard in attendance. From this moment a new policy of removing any items, from the washing line likely to be of any interest to an alcoholic hermit, was implemented whenever we went out.

Of an evening I will usually plan a cycle ride for us to complete the following day. Gill will often ask what route we are going tomorrow. In an effort to make my plan clear I might say something like " We are going out past, Lonely Girl Field." This isn't its proper name you understand it is is simply where we once saw a young woman sat on a bench on the opposite side of the field whilst we ate lunch. After half an hour or so, she got wiped a tear from her eye and walked dejectedly away. It broke my heart. Similarly we have, Fat Farmer Corner, where a corpulent gentlemen always waves to us from the comfort of a chair on the porch of his farmhouse. Requiring less explanation we also have Angry Dog Gate and Pissin Pussy Park.

Most days we will cover between twenty and forty miles on bikes. Not quite the Tour de France but challenging enough for a couple of dodgy kneed codgers in their sixties. Gill will prepare us a picnic lunch consisting of ham and cheese sandwiches, though sometimes for varieties sake we have cheese and ham. Many of the local cooked and cured meats look a little exotic for our taste so I must admit we are not very adventurous with our food.

I did once order an "Americain Filet" sandwich in a café hoping it might be a steak. It wasn't. It didn't taste that bad, although it did look a bit like mulched cold carrot. Later I was told it was raw meat so I never tried it again.

I should perhaps regard Johan as a warning to what might become of me as will be demonstrated over the next few pages. It is customary on these occasions for Gill to put a bottle of beer in the picnic for me to have with my sandwich. In the Netherlands beer is usually bought by the crate or "krat" to use the Dutch word. A "krat" contains twenty-four 30cl bottles and if you don't count the "statiegeld" or deposit will set you back around ten Euros, so it's pretty cheap.

My "krat" of choice is Heineken but there are many others. For the sake of variety, and I am more adventurous with my beer than I am my food, Gill will occasionally buy me a single bottle of something else. There is a pretty large choice when it comes to beer in the Netherlands. Some specialist shops will boast a selection of several thousand different beers and lagers. Even the local supermarket will carry quite a wide range so Gill's choice is completely random. On this occasion she selected a "Trappiste Quadrappel" It was something to do with four monks I supposed.

We set off on our cycle ride. It was a hot sunny day and after around fifteen miles of pedalling we arrived breathless, hot, hungry and thirsty at our chosen picnic spot. It was a clearing in the forest with four picnic benches, three of which were already occupied. We sat down at the one remaining bench. I poured myself a glass of the thick, brown, sweet-smelling liquid from the Trappiste Quadruppel and took a long grateful slug of it.

Now whether or not it was the heat, the fact I was hungry, or the blood pumping round my body from all the effort cycling, or a combination of all these factors I don't know, but I started to giggle. Slowly at first, but the more I tried to stop, the worse it became. Gill asked what I was laughing about, I couldn't tell her, I didn't know myself, but for some reason it was hilarious that she'd asked.

I just pointed helplessly to the beer bottle whereupon she started laughing. Well that did it, I went into the full, tickle me Elmo, Norman Wisdom Paroxysms of laughter, tears running down my face. By now we were attracting curious looks from our fellow picnicers, which I found funnier than anything in my entire life. I couldn't even perform that basic, essential to life activity of breathing in.

I've never taken illicit drugs but if what I experienced was anything like a high, I can sort of understand why some people might do it. I did eventually stop laughing. We sat and ate our sandwiches in complete ignominy, our fellow diners keeping their backs to us and studiously ignoring the weird English couple on the next table.

We set off down the cycle track in what we fervently hoped would be in the opposite direction to the others trying to enjoy their lunch and if it wasn't, then at least we could put a bit of distance between them and us.

I have a kind of classification system for Dutch cycle tracks. Most of them are very smooth concrete or tarmacadam, approximately two and half metres wide. It is like cycling across a very long billiard table. However we do sometimes come across a track that is simply made of loose stones, or worse, where the trees have rippled and torn the surface. After twenty minutes of riding down one of these you feel as if you have been buggered backwards by your bicycle saddle. If we go on too many tracks like this, it renders those of Gill's Bras not reconstructed by Johan totally wrecked. A visit to Bravissimo simply has to be regarded as a cost of the holiday. A bit like having a cars suspension repaired I suppose.

Of an evening Gill and I will often cycle a couple of miles or so up the cycle track that runs past Jan's house to the heather covered moor at the top. There we will spend a happy couple of hours or so with a bottle of wine and watch the sunset over the moorland. Often a parade of hot air balloons will float over, the silence punctuated by periodic blasts from their burners. We've also been there when dark malevolent clouds are blasted over by hurricane force winds and it rains horizontally at you.

On this one particular evening however the weather was not unpleasant so we were sat on the handily provided bench enjoying a glass of wine. Well OK then, enjoying a bottle of wine. There happened along a couple on their bicycles who I would guess were in their mid-seventies and very smartly dressed they were too. Clearly they were on their way back from church.

Here in this part of the Netherlands, the so called Bible Belt, the church reigns nearly as supremely as the bicycle. Most of the locals attend church at least twice on Sundays and the many religious holidays they have. And boy do they dress for the occasion. The women, in fine hats, tailored dresses and jackets look like they are going to a wedding. The men, in dark suits, white shirts and often black ties look like they are going to a funeral. When, at the sound of the church bells, they all walk en-masse down the main street together it really is quite a spectacular procession. Unsurprisingly Johan is nowhere to be seen.

Apologies for the slight digression, but thus attired were the couple who now stopped their bikes and stood before us as we hurriedly hid our wine glasses. He, with silver hair, worn a little longer than customary for a man of his age, an impressive but very tidy silver beard and gold pince-nez glasses looked positively beatific. A bit like I would expect a visiting deity to look if he were wanting to pay an incognito visit to Earth.

She was immaculately tailored with a perfect crown of golden hair, it would not have been difficult to see as a halo. Together they smiled at me benignly, and spoke something incomprehensible in Dutch, or perhaps it was tongues. Gill hurriedly explained that we were English, lest I embarrass her by pitching in with my, less than sober, pigeon Dutch.

"Ah ...and you are Anglicans?" he exclaimed. Before I could stop myself, I was enthusiastically declaring that we were indeed Anglicans, even though I can't remember when I last attended church. I think my slightly faulty, and it must be said alcohol fuzzed logic, thought I was confirming that we were English. "Then you are my brother" he chortled delightedly, and turning to Gill "and you my sister." He positively beamed at

Gill.

By this time my lie had been set into stone and the consequences of retracting it didn't bare thinking about, so I remained silent and smiled what I hoped was an enigmatic smile, but probably just looked pissed. I can only hope that it wasn't a visiting deity, if so the fiery furnace surely awaits me.

I would like to say that this is the only time I have gotten myself into trouble entirely of my own making, however this would be an untruth.

On another occasion, whilst we were out cycling, Gill saw a tree about twenty five metres from the cycle track with a square wrought iron fence around it. A silver plaque adorned the fence and she idly wondered about the significance of this particular tree. Interest piqued, I told her to hold the bikes, wait on the track and I would go and have a closer look.

I emerged Doctor Livingstone like, at the fence and started to decipher the text on the plaque, which told me that the tree had been planted by Queen Wilhelmina some forty years previously. I was just trying to work out what great and glorious purpose the tree in front of me was commemorating and absorbing its share of the world's excess carbon dioxide, when at the opposite side of the square fence, I spied an eye staring at me.

Unfortunately, the eye was attached to a rather large wild boar complete with impressive looking tusks. I've heard you shouldn't run, if that is sound advice, I ignored it and turned tail, carrying my feet high, to avoid tripping on the undergrowth. I looked like Shaggy from Scooby Doo running away from a ghost.

Thus I emerged, Shaggy like back at the cycle track screaming to Gill "On yer' bike and pedal like hell!" ignoring for the moment Gill's requests for further information. I never did find out what the tree was commemorating, but had I not made it, perhaps my early demise could have been added as a postscript to the plaque.

One bit of trouble which was not of my making happened as we cycled along one of the very straight and flat lanes that run across the polders. Polders are land reclaimed from the sea, they are used primarily as farming land because of the rich fertile soil. The lanes therefore are much used by tractors and other farm machinery. In the distance we saw a tractor coming towards us towing a muck spreader.

You will by now be unsurprised to learn the Dutch word is "mestverspreider". It was positively sprinting down the narrow lane and had judging by the spillage had only recently been refilled. The young driver had clearly not read the memo about being careful around bicycles and as he passed us he mestverspreidered us totally.

I fell off and shouted something not very Dutch but probably internationally understandable from the gestures I made with both hands. The tractor simply sped away. Gill caught a generous helping of sludge in her face including her mouth and nose. The following morning she was really ill and didn't recover for several days. We have since been very cautious around leaking mestverspreiders

One very hot day we set off for a cycle ride to a place called Radio Kootwijk. This is an old transmitting station dating back to before the last war when the Dutch still had colonies out in Indonesia. It broadcast Dutch language programmes to the Far East, I guess to give the colonists a small taste of home. It has long since ceased broadcasting but the building is still there, in use as a cultural, meeting and exhibition centre. A very fine piece of Art Deco architecture it is too

It is quite a long ride and so we used the main road which has a cycle track at the side of it as this was the shortest possible route. As I say it was a very hot day and cycling at the side of what is a big dual carriageway made it feel hotter still.

Presently we came upon what we took to be a garden centre, which we reasoned would have a café or snack bar. We parked our bikes and went in. The place was huge, it seemed to stock every type of garden furniture, Jacuzzi, swimming pool, summer house, green house, plant pot, outdoor textile, fountain and water feature available. Strangely there didn't seem to be a lot in the way of plants, other than those there to assist the very expensive goods that were on display look their very best.

At the centre of the enormous building were tables, each with a computer on it designed to be viewed from both sides of the table. In the centre was what I took to be a bar, but looked more like a hotel reception desk. At the far end of the bar was a fridge containing small cans of soft drinks.

I asked Gill to take a seat at one of the tables and confidently strode off in the direction of the fridge. I helped myself to a can of Coke for Gill and lemonade for myself. I walked up to person stood behind the bar. The young woman looked at me in my sweaty T-shirt and slightly grubby shorts, with a look I can only describe as a question mark.

The thing is she didn't look like she worked in a café, she was attired in a crisp white blouse, smart skirt and matching jacket with a name badge. In short she had a distinctly corporate look. She would have looked more at home behind the counter of Lloyds Bank than a café. The awful truth was beginning to dawn upon me. As I stood there with my floppy five Euro note, her quizzical expression did not change. After a moment's thought she went away, came back with two plastic cups, poured half the contents of each tin into them and placed the remainder under the counter. She then smiled brightly and said in perfect English "There's no charge sir."

I went back to the table where Gill was sat and hissed "Just drink up and let's get out of here." Gill who had been watching events unfold could not understand why from her point of view why I had paid for two cans and received only half the contents of each.

Whilst I was stood at the reception desk I had time to read the information behind. This was not a café and these were not tables intended for eating at. This was a high-end outdoor garden landscaping cum furniture supplier at which clients could sit down with an expert and plan with computer aided design technology how they were going to spend twenty or thirty thousand Euro's on making their personal outdoor space look like something from Hello Magazine.

I imagine my receptionist whilst she was wearing her question mark had an internal dialogue with herself that went something like this. "I can either explain to this sweaty little oik, in front of me that this isn't a café, but that might cause a scene in front of all these wealthy clients, or I can just give him a drink and hope that he goes away." Clearly she opted for the latter, and she was right.

One of the problems we do have staying at Jan and Tineke's is what to do with our rubbish. On a commercial site there would be large bins and recycling facilities but all our hosts have is a standard size wheelie bin. For some reason, I have never fathomed, we seem to generate huge quantities of garbage. I don't know why this should be but it seems unfair to fill their bin when they have their own waste to dispose of.

The solution we came up with was to bag it up, pop it on the back of a bike and when we come across a public litter bin, put it in. The only problem is, I'm not entirely convinced this is completely legal, so we look round for sparsely populated areas where one of us can keep look out whilst the other does the deed.

Most public litter bins are designed so as to accommodate one or two pieces of litter at a time by having a narrow slot through which to post say a drink can. Our rubbish sacks are small lilac coloured plastic bags, which I have to squeeze like a sausage through the narrow slot into the bin. If I'm ever caught I hope to convince some local authority official or maybe magistrate, that it is merely the left overs of our picnic. I suspect a quick investigation of the contents will reveal the lie.

So paranoid have we become about this that when we are followed by local authority vehicles or we see a helicopter we convince ourselves that it is all part of a sting operation to find out who is fill-ing the litter bins with bags reminiscent of lilac condoms.

For the last three years we have spent most of the summer in Elspeet, a small town between the cities of Amersfoort and Apeldoorn. We leave the caravan there and return with just the car for a few weeks to the UK periodically but between May and September we live mainly in the caravan in the Netherlands. We have become quite well known in the village. When we first get there the simple act of going to get a loaf of bread, which should take ten minutes can take upwards of an hour by the time we have exchanged a few words with the baker and all the people we have stopped to say hello to on the way there and back. But we like that, it makes us feel a part of it, a little bit more like we belong, it also does wonders for my spoken Dutch.

I now don't know how, when I was working, I drove five hundred miles there and five hundred miles back and stopped for just under two weeks, but I guess that is the advantage of being retired.

Long term caravanning does mean a bit of extra equipment like devices to attach to mains drain-age and mains water, and a portable washing machine, but there isn't a lot that you can't get for a caravan these days. You have everything that you would have in your house, it is all just a lot smaller and often a bit more delicate.

It also means a bit more planning. The bottled gas we use in the UK is not the same as that used on the continent. Well the gas may be the same, but the containers and connectors are different as is the operating pressure so they are not interchangeable. Forty odd years' membership of the EU may have given us metres, litres, and straight bananas, but you still can't buy a bottle of gas to fit your caravan over there.

As autumn closes in and the days grow shorter we start to think about leaving. It is always a sad time for us. Jan and Tineke are not getting younger and there is always the unspoken concern that we will not see them again.

We always, take coffee with them once a week and go out for a few meals with them whilst we are there. We also give a bit of the hand in the garden doing all the things that Johan should do but doesn't. Like many older people they don't have a lot of visitors and I think they look forward to the summer as much as we do. Hopefully we will soon be able to do it all again.

AND SO IT CONTINUES

I fear for my hobby in the future. I wonder if with the move to smaller engines, hybrid cars and electric vehicles if there is any place for touring caravans in the medium term.

Most electric cars seem to struggle to top a range of three hundred miles. Drop a caravan on the back and I'd be lucky to make the bottom of the Wirral. I don't think any pure electric car is yet suitable for towing with. The future also appears to be moving towards self-driving cars and I'm not sure that anyone has yet given much thought to how these would cope with a caravan. Maybe soon someone will perfect the fuel cell and all my fears will be blown away in an explosive blast of Hydrogen. In case they don't however there are a few things I'd like to do before my size ten carbon foot printed, planet destroying Volvo is banned from the road.

As for future adventures, I'd like to follow the Liberation Route all the way from the South of England to Pilsen in the Czech Republic and not put a time limit over how long we take to complete it. I would also like to go down the Rhine Valley again to Austria and maybe on into Italy, this time without the ear infection.

I did once meet a couple who had spent the whole year in their caravan touring the British Isles. They really enjoyed the lifestyle and that included spending a good chunk of the winter in Braemar Aberdeenshire, where they got trapped by the weather. That feels a bit too isolationist for me and just maybe our family would miss us.

One thing is certain though we will continue caravanning until our aching limbs and bad backs deem it to be no longer possible. For one thing it does enforce a certain level of fitness on us, I mentioned in earlier chapters the amount of work involved in caravanning. Combine it with a bit of cycling and you have no need for a gym membership.

Neither of our children have shown any interest

in caravanning. Perhaps their various crossings of the North Sea have put them off. It may just be that the world has moved on yet again whilst I wasn't looking.

Both our caravanless children, especially Phillipa, are much better travelled than we are. They have seen far more countries and experienced more different cultures than you could ever hope to in a caravan. As I also mentioned in an earlier chapter you don't see so many young families caravanning these days.

Of course I could have this very wrong indeed. It may be that as international travel becomes a more difficult and potentially dangerous occupation that the relative isolation of a caravan compared to an hotel becomes a more attractive proposition.

Developments in caravan technology are unlikely to come to a halt. In the future you may be able to go to bed in your van and wake up with it having pitched itself at some perfect location with a pub just down the road. Who knows? But if that does come to pass I would kind of miss all the hassle. For in a strange way that is what makes it such a fascinating hobby and holiday. You never do know quite what is going to happen next.

So there you have it, all my excuses laid bare. From Stony Stratford through to the Netherlands via a few places in-between. To those of you I have held up I am sorry, especially if you were on Birdlip Hill that day. To those of you who have sworn or waved at me, I could never tell quite how many fingers you were holding up, I forgive you, and I hope that you forgive me.

Printed in Great Britain
by Amazon

50322099R00147